Critical Storytelling from the Borderlands

Critical Storytelling

The titles published in this series are listed at *brill.com/csto*

Critical Storytelling from the Borderlands

En la Línea

Edited by

Carmella J. Braniger and Julio Enríquez-Ornelas

BRILL

LEIDEN | BOSTON

Cover illustration: iStock.com/FeelPic

All chapters in this book have undergone peer review.

The Library of Congress Cataloging-in-Publication Data is available online at https://catalog.loc.gov

Typeface for the Latin, Greek, and Cyrillic scripts: "Brill". See and download: brill.com/brill-typeface.

ISSN 2590-0099
ISBN 978-90-04-52113-1 (paperback)
ISBN 978-90-04-52114-8 (hardback)
ISBN 978-90-04-52115-5 (e-book)

To the undocumented around the globe

∵

Contents

Acknowledgments

We are grateful to Athena Pajer and Mallory Christenson for their help with the development stages of the project.

Figures

Notes on Contributors

Kiri Avelar

(MFA) is an interdisciplinary artist, educator, and scholar. A Jerome Robbins Dance Division Research Fellow, her scholarly research "Descubriendo Latinx: The Hidden Text in American Modern Dance" visibilizes the Latinx diasporic presence in the early American modern dance canon. Her correlating artistic practice is designed to further provoke thought around the artistic, physical, and cultural borderless experience of Latinx artists in America, and immerses audiences in unique spaces to explore themes of ruido, mestiza consciousness, intersectionality, migration, and Latinidades through film, embodied oral history performances, interactive screendance, and soundscapes. She is co-founder of two creative learning sites, the Latinx Dance Educators Alliance, a resource center for dance educators, and ColectivXs, an interdisciplinary artist collective. Hecha en las fronteras de El Paso, Texas/Ciudad Juárez, Chihuahua, Mexico, she currently resides in New York City.

Irving Ayala

was born in 1999 in Cojutepeque, El Salvador. Growing up, he was fascinated with storytelling, and this interest led to some early exposure to reading since his mother keep feeding him books as gifts. Later, at the age of 15 Ayala migrated to Virginia. In "Todo en una maleta," Irving explores the story of immigration through Rome and how these events are repeated across history. Irving draws inspiration from his own story and projects it in the story with the narrator. "Todo en una maleta" is Ayala's first published work.

Carmella J. Braniger

is a Professor of English at Millikin University, where she teaches creative writing and literature. She has published several narrative poems, over fifty micropoems, and more than a dozen poetry sequences which have appeared in *Sycamore Review*; *MARGIE: The American Journal of Poetry*; *Modern English Tanka*; *Altas Poetica*, and others. Her chapbook, *No One May Follow*, was published by Pudding House Publications in 2009. More recently, her research and artistic achievement energies have focused on Brill's Critical Storytelling series, which provides a platform for marginalized voices to tell stories about and advocate equal access and opportunity for excluded identities. Contributing to this venture has allowed her to integrate issues of diversity and inclusivity into her scholarly efforts. She currently serves as the Distinguished Warren F. Hardy Professor of English and looks forward to researching narrative testimony and poetry of witness as genres for processing and sharing our traumatic pasts.

Roxana Fragoso Carrillo

was born in Hermosillo, Sonora, México. She has a bachelor's degree in Hispanic Literatures from the University of Sonora, as well as a master's degree in Hispanoamerican Literature from the same institution. She is an editor of commercial journal, a teacher of high school and college students, and a co-author of the textbook *Taller de Lectura y Redacción 11*, published by Gafra editores. Currently, she is a Social Sciences Ph.D. student at the Colegio de Sonora (in Historic Studies about Regiom and Border) and her thesis is called 'Frontera y memoria en la narrativa de Miguel Méndez' [Border and Memory on Miguel Mendez's Narrative].

Marisa V. Cervantes

is a Chicana from East Palo Alto, CA, and is the first in her family to go to college. She is currently a doctoral candidate at Washington State University in the Department of Sociology. Her research interests are centered in racial/ethnic identity among Latinxs, young adulthood, Chicana feminism, and the experiences of minoritized students in historically white institutions of higher education. While Marisa teaches sociology classes in the college setting, she is a firm believer that education can happen anywhere, not just in the classroom. She is proud to be able to share her knowledge with family who did not have the opportunity to pursue formalized education, as their sacrifices have granted her the privilege of becoming a (soon to be!) Doctora.

Guadalupe Chavez

is a Ph.D. student in the Department of Politics and International Relations at the University of Oxford. Her project exams how countries of origin manage the influx of returnees and why return migration policies vary across and within countries over time with a focus on Latin America. More broadly, her research interests include international migration, citizenship regimes, political economy and diaspora politics. Guadalupe received her Master's from the New School for Social Research and was a 2018–2019 Fulbright scholar in Mexico, where she explored the political struggles and demands that arise in the aftermath of deportation.

Julio Enríquez-Ornelas

is a writer and literary critic. He completed a double major in English and Spanish literature at Wabash College, earned an M.A. in Hispanic Studies from the University of California Riverside, and completed a Ph.D. in Latin American Literature and Culture from the University of California-Riverside. His academic work is rooted in examining transnational diasporas at the margins of Latin American, Latinx, and Mexican Studies. His critical and creative work has appeared in *Hispania, Journal of the Midwest Modern Language Association*, *Textos Híbridos*, *Alchemy: Journal of Translation* and others. His most recent peer-reviewed article, "Troubling border representations in Mexican cultural studies and U.S. Central American cultural studies" appears in *Prose Studies: History, Theory, and Criticism*. Currently, he chairs the Department of Modern Languages and coordinates the Global Studies program at Millikin University where he teaches Spanish.

Liliana Conlisk Gallegos

is a performer of research, a translator, and an uncivil disruptor who doesn't know her place. She is a filter that collects, isolates, and exposes supremacist formats while designing hubs to compile digital and analogue collections of designs. As an Optimus Prime Trauma Transformer con lengua de machete, Liliana Conlisk Gallegos cannot help but experiment with EVERYTHING including art, virtual reality, and all forms of media. Her live, interactive media art production and rasquache performances generate culturally specific, collective, technocultural creative spaces of production that reconnect Chicana/o/x Mestiza Indigenous wisdom and conocimiento to their ongoing technological and scientific contributions. As a transfronteriza (perpetual border crosser), the current limited perceptions of what research, media, and technology can be and do are like a yonke (junkyard), from which pieces are upcycled and repurposed to amplify individual and collective expression, community healing, and social justice.

Lina Paredes Espitia

is an audiovisual professional and web developer junior, with experience in events management and social media. As a creative person she is always on the search for new challenges. She has spent her working years as a community manager, where she expanded her writing abilities, learned about SEO and meetings with clients, and helped to manage language exchange events, which she hosted, planned, and developed both online and outdoors.

Verónica Gaona

was born in Brownsville, Texas and is an interdisciplinary artist and educator living and working between Texas and Tamaulipas. Through sculpture, installation, and digital media her work looks at the shifting and multiple spaces at the border to better understand the complexities of contradictory forces. In 2019, she traveled to Marfa, Paris and Nantes, France to take part in DUST, a residency working at the intersection of spatial practice, critical theory, and contemporary art. In August of 2021, she exhibited at the Museum of

Contemporary Art of Tamaulipas in México. She holds a Master of Fine Arts in Studio Art with a concentration in photography and digital media and is currently an adjunct professor at the University of Houston.

Andrea Gómez

is a Peruvian anthropologist focused on body, beauty and gender studies, researching the cosmetic industry in Peru and Mexico. She obtained her Ph.D. in Anthropology from the Universidad Autónoma Metropolitana – Iztapalapa in Mexico City. A non-fiction writer, she writes about the multiple realities and inequalities experienced as a feminist and autistic woman. She also has an activist background on sexual and reproductive health, anti-racism, and neurodiversity.

Filiberto Mares Hernández

was born in El Guayabo, Ayotlán Jalisco, México. He teaches Hispanic linguistics and Spanish courses at Benedictine College, in Atchison Kansas. Filiberto has published poetry, short stories, and academic articles related to Latin American literature and film. In 2017 he published his first novel, *El maíz y tú.*

Víctor M. Macías-González

is Professor of History and Women's, Gender, and Sexuality Studies at the University of Wisconsin, La Crosse, where he serves as Faculty Fellow for Diversity, Inclusion, and Internationalization in the College of Arts, Social Studies, and Humanities. A native of El Paso, Texas, Macías-González grew up in Ciudad Juárez, Chihuahua. He received his doctorate in Latin American History and Letters from Texas Christian University in 1999. His research interests are the history of masculinity and homosexuality, and nineteenth century Mexican history. He has published dozens of articles and book chapters, coedited, with Anne Rubenstein, *Masculinity and Sexuality in Modern Mexico* (University of New Mexico Press, 2012) and is presently working on a book on Mexico's first transwoman, Martha Olmos Romero (1932–1972) and on a monograph on domesticity and the emergence of the homophile movement in Mexico ca. 1930–1970.

Carol Mariano

was born on the island of Mindanao, Philippines and migrated with her family to Australia in her teens. She is an explorer at heart with a deep-seated curiosity to understand the similarities and differences of human realities and through her personal experience, Mariano attempts to translate impressions and symbolic meanings into a wide-range of artistic practices: experimental film, digital art, writing, art journaling, and sound. Her approach deals with issues of identity and displacement—exploring the idea of the contemporary self and its boundaries between the personal and the political. Mariano completed a Bachelor of Arts in Creative Arts with First Class Honours at Griffith University and is currently pursuing a counselling degree with her old alma mater.

Ana Silvia Monzón Monterroso

is a sociologist and feminist communicator, professor, and researcher in gender studies and feminisms at FLACSO-Guatemala. Co-founder of Voces de Mujeres, Mujeres Abriendo Caminos and other feminist communication spaces, they work on issues related to women's history, gender and migration, communication, education, and sexuality. They are a member of the University Commission for Women-USAC and the GT Feminisms, resistance, and emancipation.

Juana Moriel-Payne

was born and raised in Ciudad Juárez, a border city with El Paso. Her creative writing reflects her experience living in this complex area. Her poetry reflects her observations about women's issues. She holds an MA in Hispanic literature and a PhD in Borderlands history. She is a published novelist and currently she is translating one of her novels to English and writing a novella. She is a professor at Mount Saint Mary's University–Los Angeles and director of the Latin America and Latinx Creative Studies Certificate in the MFA Creative Writing Program.

Rachel Neff

has written poetry since elementary school and has notebooks full of half-written novels. She earned her doctorate in Spanish literature and holds an MFA. Her work has been published in *JuxtaProse Magazine*, *Crab Fat Magazine* and included in several anthologies. Her books include *The Haywire Heart and Other Musings on Love* and *Chasing Chickens: When Life after Higher Education Doesn't Go the Way You Planned*.

Jumko Ogata-Aguilar

is an AfroJapanese and pocha writer from Veracruz, Mexico. She studied an undergraduate degree in Latin American Studies at UNAM (Universidad Autónoma de México). She writes fiction, essays, and film criticism, has been published by Revista de la Universidad, Vogue Mexico and the British Council of Mexico, and is currently a columnist for CoolHuntermx. Her work focuses on identity, collective memory, racialization and racism in Mexico. She has taught antiracism workshops for Facebook, Twitter, Mexico's Department of Culture as well as non-profits in Mexico and the US.

José Olivarez

is the son of Mexican immigrants. His debut book of poems, Citizen Illegal, was a finalist for the PEN/Jean Stein Award and a winner of the 2018 Chicago Review of Books Poetry Prize. It was named a top book of 2018 by The Adroit Journal, NPR, and the New York Public Library. Along with Felicia Chavez and Willie Perdomo, he co-edited the poetry anthology, *The BreakBeat Poets Vol. 4: LatiNEXT*. He is the co-host of the poetry podcast, The Poetry Gods. In 2018, he was awarded the first annual Author and Artist in Justice Award from the Phillips Brooks House Association and named a Debut Poet of 2018 by Poets & Writers. In 2019, he was awarded a Ruth Lilly and Dorothy Sargent Rosenberg Poetry Fellowship from the Poetry Foundation. His work has been featured in *The New York Times*, *The Paris Review*, and elsewhere.

Isabela Ortega

is a New Mexico raised artist based in Albuquerque, NM and Chicago, IL. Her Chicana identity has inspired her to be artistically and musically inclined since childhood. She attended Highland High School and other public institutions in New Mexico's most diverse community, the International District, and takes great pride in her "war zone" roots despite its adversity. She is an alum of The Oxbow School's 41st semester in Napa, California, and is currently obtaining a Bachelor of Fine Arts with an Emphasis in Writing at the School of the Art Institute of Chicago. Frequent trips to visit loved ones in Chihuahua, Mexico led to her profound appreciation for the borderlands and its complexities. Social justice, death, domesticity and contemporary motifs are explored through her multidisciplinary art practice, often inspired by storytelling and symbolism in the mundane.

Paul Pedroza

was born and raised in El Paso, Texas. He received his M.F.A. in Fiction from the University of Illinois at Urbana-Champaign. His story collection, *The Dead Will Rise and Save Us*, is available from Veliz Books. He has completed his first novel, and he is currently working on a second along with a collection of essays. His work has appeared in *Rattle*, *MAKE: A Chicago Literary Magazine*, *Palabra*, *Confluencia*, *Inquiring Mind Buddhist Magazine*, and in the following anthologies: *Our Lost Border* (Arte Público Press), *New Border Voices* (TAMU Press), and *Mezcla 2* (Tumblewords).

Jorge Omar Ramírez Pimienta

is an artist/writer/scholar who lives and works in the San Diego/Tijuana border region. His artistic practice examines questions of identity, trans-nationality, emergency poetics, landscape and memory. He holds a PhD in Literature from the University of California San Diego and a MFA in Visual Arts from the same institution. He is currently member of the Mexican Sistema Nacional de Creadores de Arte in the area of poetry.

Raphaella Prange

was a first-generation college student and the child of a Latin-American immigrant. She earned her Bachelor's of Arts Degree in Interpersonal Communication from DePauw University (Greencastle, IN) and her Master's of Science Degree in Student Affairs Administration from Indiana State University (Terre Haute, IN). She currently serves as the Vice President for Student Affairs at Millikin University. Raphaella is also a Court Appointed Special Advocate for Macon County, a board member for the Children's Museum of Illinois, a member of the Illinois Energy Assistance Commission, and volunteers for Decatur Public Schools in parent engagement and magnet school initiatives. Passionate about making a difference in the lives of youth, Raphaella has bloomed where she has been planted. As a proud Decatur, Illinois resident, she lives in the historic west end on an urban microfarm homestead with her husband Rob and two children, Robert (16) and Suzanne (14).

Felipe Quetzalcoatl Quintanilla

was born in Mexico City to a Mexican mother and a Salvadoran father. Quintanilla emigrated to Canada at the age of ten. His creative works have been included in several print anthologies as well as in various online publications. He is also currently an Assistant Professor of Hispanic Studies at Western University.

Erica Reyes

is a BFA Art Therapy Major at Millikin University. Her concentrations are Drawing and Photography. Through these mediums, she seeks to project emotions onto the audience to evoke uncomfortable feelings. She likes to present issues often ignored in society, forcing the subjects to be talked about. She has recently put more focus into self-portraits as she works to create a deeper connection with her audience.

Fidel García Reyes

was born in Guerrero, México. He completed a Master's in Gender Studies at El Colegio de México (Mexico City) and moved to the U.S. in 2016. Fidel is also a fiction writer. He has published numerous short stories and his first novel, *La estatua de Azúcar*, was published in 2017. He is currently a Ph.D. student at UT-Austin in the Department of Spanish and Portuguese.

Lizbeth De La Cruz Santana

is a first generation Latinx student of color and a Ph.D. candidate in Spanish Latin American Literatures and Cultures at UC Davis. Her doctoral dissertation centers on the deportation of US childhood arrivals to Mexico and identifies a range of ethical-oriented concerns regarding the legal treatment of this group. In her dissertation, she coins the Childhood Arrivals Critical Theory (CACrit) framework, the childhood arrivals Diaspora, and introduces a more general definition of this group.

Santiago Vaquera-Vasquez

is an unrepentant border crosser, writer, painter, former DJ, and academic who has published stories in international literary journals and newspapers as well as in major anthologies on contemporary literature in the Americas. He has been invited to give readings from his work at universities and conferences in Spain, Mexico, Colombia, and the United States. Currently an assistant professor in the Department of Spanish and Portuguese at the University of Iowa, he has also taught at Penn State, Texas A & M University, and has been a visiting scholar at Dartmouth College. In 2006, as a Fulbright Senior Lecturer in Spain, he lectured at universities in Madrid and Salamanca. His academic work on US/Mexico border cultures has been published in journals and anthologies in Mexico and the United States.

Introduction

Carmella J. Braniger and Julio Enríquez-Ornelas

> Before turning our eyes 'forward' let's cast a look at the roads that
> led us here.
>
> GLORIA ANZALDÚA ("Acts of Healing," 2015, p. XXVII)

∴

In her essay "Acts of Healing" from *This Bridge Called My Back*, Gloria Anzaldúa
emphasizes how important it is to look back and build bridges with the past
as we push forward in the fight against oppression. In her landmark book *The
Borderlands: La Frontera*, Anzaldúa (2012) frames language as a means for
invoking art from everyday life. She recalls a time before, when "poets gath-
ered to play music, dance, sing and read poems in open-air places," and, in her
writing, she celebrates "the ability of story ... to transform the storyteller and
the listener" (p. 88). Stories are the catalyst of change, which begins with the
interaction between the speaker's utterance and the audience's willingness to
listen. Storytelling is an ancient social and aesthetic act that draws in others.
Through the enactment of story, the storyteller works to sustain cultural imagination while also affirming his own experience and even existence.

The authors published in *Critical Storytelling from the Borderlands* invoke
and enact story by using multimodal composition techniques to create new
knowledge about crossing borders. This invocation takes the form of various
modes of representation from poetry to photography, autoethnography to
installation art, micro-fictions to memoir. As the authors of this volume cor-
respond with Anzaldúa, they engage in the ethnopoetic and performative act
of storytelling in the name of social justice. From feminists writing in response
to Andzaldúa's call to action to nomadic artists crafting representations of border life as constant movement and identity shifting, this collection contains
rebellious voices and projects that seek to doubt and even subvert common
sense, question the status quo, and tear down regimes of domination all while
envisioning possibilities for change.

∴

DOI:10.1163/9789004521155_001

As Andzaldúa first uttered, we use this introduction to look back at the pathways that lead us here to the publication of this book. As we journey through the past recollecting our aims and intentions, the storytellers carve new routes of possibility for borderland studies. The first story that sparked this volume began back in 2019. On June 22 of that year, Julio Enríquez-Ornelas published his critical story "America, are you great again?" on Facebook:

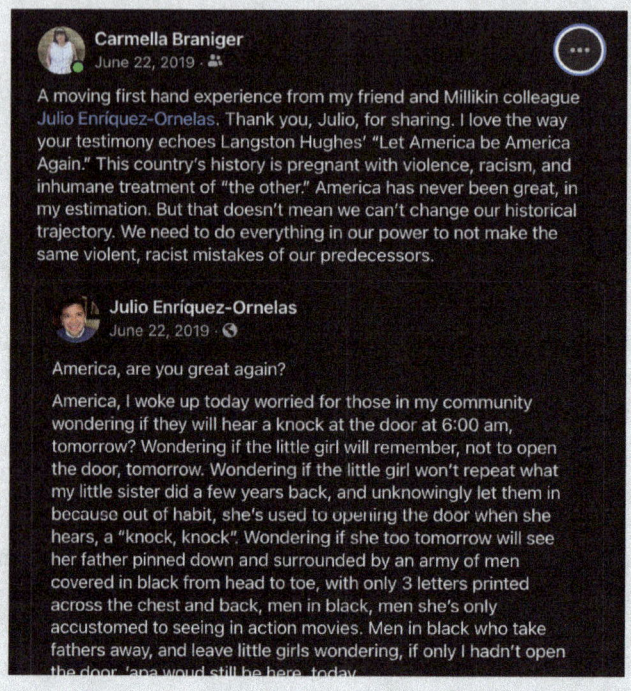

America, I woke up today worried for those in my community wondering if they will hear a knock at the door at 6:00 am, tomorrow? Wondering if the little girl will remember, not to open the door, tomorrow. Wondering if the little girl won't repeat what my little sister did a few years back, and unknowingly let them in because out of habit, she's used to opening the door when she hears, a "knock, knock". Wondering if she too tomorrow will see her father pinned down and surrounded by an army of men covered in black from head to toe, with only 3 letters printed across the chest and back, men in black, men she's only accustomed to seeing in action movies. Men in black who take fathers away, and leave little girls wondering, if only I hadn't opened the door, 'apa would still be here, today.

America, how many more families need to be separated until we're great again? How many more children will need to be torn apart from their parents? You already did it to my family, you already took my step-dad, and we're rebuilding, trying harder than ever to reach some type of American Dream, if it still exists for people like me, people like you, people like us. America, are you great since you took him? Are things getting back to this nostalgic imagination of the past, of what America once was, and no longer is because the rest of the world no longer is either because the times are changing, the world is changing, and we must too, and deporting people who look like me will not make you great again.

Last night I went to bed wondering who is next? Will friends be gone, tomorrow? Will a family member have to resettle unexpectedly, tomorrow? Will them losing their job, home, and family make this country great again? Last night, I went to bed seeing the young and brilliant undocumented and unafraid poets, afraid, trying so hard to be positive, trying so hard to push forward, and not let this hateful rhetoric get the best of them, and seeing them afraid, seeing them more cautious of who can see them...America, are you great again?

Last night I went to bed wondering if the DACA program will be? Last night I went to bed thinking of all the hardworking and gifted gente serving as professors and scholars, wondering what will be of them if they won't be able to renew their status? And in this current political climate they too are wondering, perhaps, like me if they are next, will they be next on the list of collateral bodies, as part of some agenda and plan to make you great again. America, when will I be next? America, since you began taking human rights away from women are you great again? America, since you began taking the right to be and love for all humans, are you great again? So, tell me America, are you? I'm truly wondering what more do we need to lose until we get to that imagined greatness? America, how many more rights and people will need to be lost until you are great again.

In the opening line of this post, "America, are you great again?," Enríquez-Ornelas echoes Langston Hughes' poem "Let America be America Again," as well as that poem's refrain "America never was America to me" creating his own lament for a dream deferred. The prose post goes on to deliver a rather repetitive and cadenced rendition of a *call-out* as well as a call *for* revision of the American dream. Like Hughes, Enríquez-Ornelas outlines the ways in which he has limited access to privileges taken for granted by most white Americans: safety, security, a job, a home, a family. From Hughes to Enríquez-Ornelas, the construction, deconstruction, and reconstruction of the American dream permeates our literature. In dialogue with other early American writers like Alexis De Tocqueville, Enríquez-Ornelas "wonders" about and interrogates the concept of "greatness," an American ideal brought into the mainstream by president Donald Trump, whose slogan for his 2016 campaign was "make American great again." He pleads with his country "America, how many more families need to be separated until we're great again?"

Just as America "never was America" for Hughes, Enríquez-Ornelas suggests that America never was great, particularly for immigrants, so how could it be great "again." "How many more?" he asks, "How many children and families must suffer, how many more lives will be ruined, how many more lives lost." Enríquez-Ornelas truly wonders "what more do we need to lose until we get to that imagined greatness." Both Hughes and Enríquez-Ornelas imagine an America not meant for them though neither gives up hope that life can and will be better in America if we continue to fight for the rights and freedom of all. Enríquez-Ornelas warns that "times are changing, the world is changing, and we must too, and deporting people who look like me will not make you great again." If Hughes asks us all to dream of better—better jobs, better homes, better lives—then Enríquez-Ornelas reminds us that better is never better for all and always worse for some.

Immediately after reading Enríquez-Ornelas's post, I met with him, and we began collaborating on a volume for the Critical Storytelling series with Brill, a series I helped colleagues Brandon Hensley and Nicholas Hartlep launch several years back. As I explained when we met, critical storytellers provoke readers to acknowledge and question different perspectives. Critical storytelling questions unquestioned norms and assumptions imposed by those in power. It envisions possibilities for change. It exposes oppression in its various forms. Critical storytellers voice silences and rely on diverse storytelling methods, theoretical approaches, and narrative frameworks to offer new stories that are critical of exclusionary and divisive metanarratives. Critical stories are counternarratives that focus on a moment of personal transformation, but subjective experiences do not operate in a vacuum. Such qualitative inquiry can help us understand the lives of authors who are brave enough to write their stories, and in doing so to fight what Paulo Freire refers to in his landmark study *Pedagogy of the Oppressed* as the "naïve consciousness," and to instead raise critical and political awareness (1972). Such stories provide a space for marginalized, silenced community voices to seek external resonance and validation through ethnographic social justice storytelling.

∴

Often, those in power use language to dictate cultural values, and for Anzaldúa this is true in both English and Spanish. If you do not possess the language of power, then you go unheard. This exclusionary use of language leads to stories told only from the perspective of those who speak the primary language. In other words, misrepresentations of historically colonized, marginalized, or excluded people result when the language of power is only utilized by those in power to speak of and for those who are unable to use English to utter their story. Gloria Anzaldúa's work was revolutionary during her time because she combated misrepresentation and exclusion with her revolutionary use of languages. She affirms, "... I am my own language. Until I can take pride in my language, I cannot take pride in myself" (2012, p. 81). Later Gloria Anzaldúa states, "Until I am free to write bilingually and to switch codes without having always to translate, while I still have to speak English or Spanish when I would rather speak Spanglish, and as long as I have to accommodate the English speakers rather than having them accommodate me, my tongue will be illegitimate. I will no longer be made to feel ashamed for existing. I will hear my voice" (2012, p. 81). For speakers of marginalized languages, we are unwillingly ascribing a narrative as imagined by a white gaze rooted in the English language.

Published writing by the global majority is not in dialogue with the language of power of the present: English. The inability of the global majority to fully take part in the dominant print narrative can generate a sense of disarticulation, or, if one is able to take part in the dominant print narrative, it's only after assimilating normative forms of speech. All of this just so one's words can be seen and heard. If one's experience is seen and heard, then it implies the experience exists. Hence, writing becomes an act of making seen the invisible. For Gloria Anzaldúa, this meant affirming, "I will overcome the tradition of silence" (2012, p. 81). Her use of language was nonexistent. Neither at home nor elsewhere was there a place for Anzaldúa to speak and be heard, not even when writing. She was completely displaced. Her empowerment came with her recognition of this imposed silence and then speaking up against it with her own language—Spanglish. Her language became her tool for survival and say, "No, this must end. That is not my experience," or, to echo what Nobel Peace Prize winner Rigoberta Menchú once said to Elisabeth Burgos-Debray, "Yo soy Rigoberta Menchú y así nació mi conciencia."

In her writing, it is clear Anzaldúa does not follow any preconceived writing tradition, especially in terms of form and content, which then was and now continues to be revolutionary. Perhaps now the content has changed, but her form remains. Anzaldúa (2012) explains her work to readers:

In looking at this book that I'm almost finished writing, I see a mosaic pattern (Aztec-like) emerging, a weaving pattern, thin here, thick there. I see a preoccupation with the deep structure, the underlying structure, with the gesso underpainting that is red earth, black earth. I can see the deep structure, the scaffolding. If I can get the bone structure right, then putting flesh on it proceeds without too many hitches. The problem is that the bones often do not exist prior to the flesh but are shaped after a vague shadow of its form is discerned or uncovered during beginning, middle and final stages of writing. (p. 88)

In *Critical Storytelling from the Borderlands*, writers turn to Anzaldúa's work not as a point of contention or celebration of her words, but rather as a point for departure in how we make sense of the borderlands in the 21st century. In some ways, the artists in this book are on a path first paved by Anzaldúa, but they come with different spectacles. The form of our book itself and the work of many of the contributors are part of the same collective experience captured in Anzaldúa's book, which is the spectacle of cultural survival. The work of many contributors in this volume speaks of the structural, every day, symbolic, and political violence that comes with being deemed other based on language, race, gender, sexuality, or social class. The back and forth of cultural survival—of trying to be as you are, while simultaneously being erased or modified to fit in—can be understood as a contested space at the borderline. When thinking about borderlands, Gloria Anzaldúa's work is crucial especially when it comes to giving visibility to her experience as an embodiment of how people are colonized by the culture of another, while simultaneously being oppressed. For Anzaldúa the plot of land known as the U.S./México border is the borderlands; it is where English and Spanish come together and give way to unique cultural representations. Without Gloria Anzaldúa's interdisciplinary masterpiece, *Borderlands/La Frontera: The New Mestiza* there would be no *Critical Storytelling from the Borderlands*.

∴

The stories in this volume are the result of considering the scope of the critical story and casting an inclusive net for narratives on borderland dwelling. From meditations on the geographical border, "la lína," to representations of resistance, pain, violence, womanhood, and memory, this collection features various emerging and established autonomous voices who tell their borderlands stories. Each contributor works diligently to situate and contextualize their personal subjectivities and transformations within the larger culture(s) of borders. These voices use gestural, spatial, aural, visual, and linguistic modes to empower themselves against oppressive environments and to create counternarratives in which ethnographic social justice storytelling takes place.

The opening piece of Part 1, "En La Línea," is an autoethnography "Remember, Roots Still Grow Beneath" from the scholar and artist Liliana Conlisk Gallegos, who defines in language—both English and Spanish—as well as visually the border crosser as a "conscious transfronteriza/o/x," who experiences trauma and invisibility in their struggle to survive. Turning to their own history, they make new knowledge about the impact of the border on those who cross it daily and Conlisk Gallegos makes a call to action for her readers to do the same. Then, in the beautifully written historical memoir "Life on the U.S.-Mexico border, 1970–1980," Víctor M. Macías-González recalls the stories of their lived experience at the border as a child. According to his essay "Field Notes from the Borderlands," Santiago Vaquera-Vásquez was "born a Mexican in the United States." His autoethnographic piece opens and closes with a shout-out to border dwellers to unite. Vaquera-Vásquez documents a lifetime of crossing borders from the details of their passport to the names on the wall at Tijuana. Reflecting on the role of storytelling, they add their own stories to the cacophony of voices who have come before. Lizbeth De La Cruz Santana in *"The Playas de Tijuana Mural Project*: Digital Storytelling, Portraiture and U.S.-México Border Art" takes a multifaceted approach to storytelling using digital activism, portraiture, art, and technology in order to take back the wall. By reclaiming and repurposing a space connected to "violence, death, human rights violations" they attempt to enable migration and enact the inclusion of the immigrant experience.

In the second part of the book, "Wild Tongues" are works that embody personal, first-person point of view accounts that refuse to be silenced or tamed. In their autoethnography "Criterion Number 3: Unstable Sense of Self; ca. 1993," Paul Pedroza chronicles their identity struggles with obesity, borderline personality disorder, and their Mexican-American heritage. Jumko Ogata-Aguilar in their ethnographic prose offers a lens into life in Mexico City via Chicanxs living in the United States. In their ethnographic essay 我, 外国女人, "Me, Foreign Woman," Andrea Gómez offers a perspective of a human who seeks survival through educational opportunity in Paris, France, and later São Paolo Brazil, all while encountering various forms of microaggressions and racism rooted in social class. Spanish literature scholar and poet Rachel Neff mixes the genres of the academic essay, personal memoir, and poetry to explore the borders of the word "Liminality," which is the title of their piece. They brilliantly guide the reader through the terrain of memory and language as they detail their journey in resisting categorizations of identity. Ana Silvia Monzón Monterroso writes two ethnographic poems in Spanish. In the first one, "Feminista" there is an emphasis on affirming and detailing their feminist perspective rooted, which ends with two questions, what is a feminist and what is a woman, and not who.

The third part of the book, "Thin Edge of Barbwire," brings together representations of the border in which pain and violence abound. Poet and artist Jorge Omar Ramírez Pimienta presents their poetry, photography, and installation art as commentaries on migration and deportation. In their work from *Albums of Fences*, they create a character to explore border identity. "Welcome to Colonia Libertad" extends their critique of American ideals and reveals the deflated reality of liberty for all. Filiberto Mares Hernández's "Salamandra" is flash fiction in Spanish rooted in a Latin American literary tradition in terms of the narrative aesthetic. In it, the main character and daughter wait to cross, all while memory and technology merge through the inclusion of colloquial language found on Facebook and bouts of stream of consciousness. Isabela Ortega's two visual collages create a Memoriam for those lost in the El Paso Walmart shooting. A response to poet Elizabeth Bishop, "Heart of the Borderland" explores themes of loss and longing. In "La Rosa de El Paso," Ortega sources photos taken at the memorial to arrange a symbolic representation of imprecation, which they suggest is responsible for the shooting. In his poem "My Friends from Work," Fidel García Reyes expresses the pain and vulnerability of immigrant workers whose lives depend on daily border crossing, their lives constantly a walk along the thin edge of barbwire Anzaldúa describes. Veronica Gaona's collection of photographs, *Las casas y nosotros* aims at exploring how memory and time are present in the in *builtarquitectures* in Valle Hermoso, Tamaulipas near the Rio Grande Valley. Their photos examine the relationship of "architecture, migration, and death in the context of transnational relationships within the remittance landscape." A Mexican American raised in America and a student at Millikin University, Erica Reyes delves into the binary aspect of their identity in their charcoal and pastel self-portrait entitled "I Am Enough." Their representation is reminiscent of Frida Kahlo's self-portraits and suggests the paradox of identity experienced by border dwellers.

In the fourth part, "Shadow Beast" we bring together representations of womanhood affirmed. In Marisa V. Cervantes' "That's Not my Name: A Journey of Reclamation" the powerful voice of this prose seeks to take ownership of their name and delineates with personal memory and lived cultural experience how the constant mis-representation of her name is an act of violence. In their academic Spanish essay *"Este puente/mi espalda*: Interseccionalidad entre feminismo y chicanismo," Roxana Fragoso Carrillo traces Chicana feminism and positions it as translational knowledge impacting feminist thought in Mexico, all with the goal of confronting, "nuestro propio racismo." Juana Moriel-Payne writes two ethnographic poems and a microfiction in Spanish, in one poem, there is an emphasis on the women who stay home waiting for their loved ones to come back home from their journey to the United States. In the microfiction piece, the focus on women remains, and rather than the woman who sits and waits, and longs for loved ones, the focus is on domestic workers; women crossing the Paso del Norte International Bridge, which crosses the Rio Grande connecting the United States-Mexico border cities of El Paso, Texas, and Ciudad Juárez, Chihuahua. Kiri Avelar's visual art *Cilantro Taconeo, Manos de Maiz,* and *Texas Masa* is influenced by Gloria Anzaldúa and Michelle Manzanales. Their work embodies the intersection of notions of *ruido*, Mestiza Consciousness, migration, and Latinidad. Overall, their work seeks to "consider gestures, symbols, and sounds that speak to the in-between space." Carol Mariano's *Shadows Series* questions boundaries by experimenting with abstract black and white silhouette representations of the self/other tensions of border existence, arriving at the conclusion that border dwellers are fragmented selves, always lacking completion.

In the last part, "Writing as a Sensuous Act," we bring together nonfiction pieces that explore what it means to forget in the past, present, and future. In "Todo en una maleta," Irving Ayala writes a science-fiction short story in Spanish set in the future. In his poem, "when i say diaspora," José Olivarez explores the nuances and paradox of what it means to experience dispersion from an original homeland. Second-generation American Latina Raphaella Prange explores the memory and meaning of a pair of navy-blue boots that shaped their identity early on. She seeks to reconnect with her culture and history in her autobiographical essay "Hecho a Mano, Made by Hand." In Felipe Quetzalcoatl Quintanilla's Spanish short story, "La Chip Truck," the narrator takes readers to Leamington, Canada; a town Miles away from the U.S. Canada Border in Detroit, Michigan. In this work of creative nonfiction, the narrative voice details the journey of a Mexican immigrant family working toward a better life, all while experiencing various forms of racism and discrimination. In poetic prose "solo jeans," "over sopes and burritos," "My first language is Spanish," and "dolar," Julio Eníquez-Ornelas tells stories that reveal the subtle nuances of his hybrid identity as a "pre-dreamer." With vulnerability, they question America's stance on immigration, establish Spanglish as their official language of expression, and make resolutions for a world without borders. We close the volume with the interview "Coloniality Incarnate: Conversational Assemblage with Liliana Conlisk Gallegos, Jorge Omar Ramírez Pimienta, and Julio Enríquez-Ornelas" featuring Carmella Braniger engaging with three border crossers.

∴

"If only" (¡Ojalá!) is the response to the opening question of Luis Felipe Lomelì's micro-narrative "El Emigrante": "Forget anything?" (¿Olvida usted algo?). Many of the authors published in *Critical Storytelling from the Borderlands* have left behind love, land, family, loneliness, violence, and even parts of self and identity. Broken spirits like bones heal and move on, but that does not mean what is left behind is forgotten. Rather than forget what we leave behind, we remember even and especially what we've not taken with us. We carry with us our personal and collective histories when we cross borders. Even more than recollecting our own memories as we cross into new spaces, we are also always gleaning and re-assembling the collective memory of what remains behind.

As we build bridges with the past and push forward in the fight against oppression, we fight to recover the stories of those we lost, those forgotten so that we can continue to add meaning to that loss, and so that we can live new stories into the future. We tell our stories to make and build new community beyond borders and to ignite change for which to prepare we must, like the ancients, gather at the table, as if it were a bonfire, with the only task to tell new stories constructed from the shattered pieces of liminal borderland experiences. This collective act of evolving memory by telling the stories of our minds, bodies, and lands, esto es crear a new consciousness—*una conci-enda de mujer*—a consciousness of the borderlands. As you turn each page of this book, listen to the swell of voices as they emerge from this new *mestiza* consciousness.

References

Anzaldùa, G. (2012). *Borderlands: Las frontera: The new Mestiza* (4th ed.). Aunt Lute.

Anzaldùa, G. (2015). Acts of healing. In C. Moraga & G. Andzaldùa (Eds.), *This bridge called my back: Writings by radical women of color* (4th ed.; pp. xvii–xxviii). SUNY.

Enríquez-Ornelas, J. (2019, June 22). America, are you great again? *Facebook.*

Freire, P. (1972). *Pedagogy of the oppressed.* Penguin.

Hughes, L. (1994). Let America be America again. In *The collected poems of Langston Hughes* (pp. 189–191). Vintage.

Lomeli, L. F. (2005). El emigrante. In *Ella sigue de viaje* (p. 1). Tusquets Editores.

PART 1

En La Línea

∴

CHAPTER 1

Remember, Roots Still Grow Beneath

Learning from Conscious Transfronteriza/o/x *Trauma*

Liliana Conlisk Gallegos

Es que la neta, está cañón escribir esto because I want to share about some of the hidden wounds that people like me, conscious *transfronterizos*, carry forever. Norma Iglesias Prieto (2004) writes that conscious *transfronterizos* have a hard time healing because their struggle can be imperceptible, apparently insignificant in its quotidian invisibility. *Y así, insignificantemente* with each violent attack, with each child separated from their families, each macro and micro-aggression experienced, each act of violence and dehumanization, *se encarna y remueve la herida abierta de la que habla Gloria Anzaldúa; con cada rajada.*

FIGURE 1.1   "Precious lunar self-portrait – The Coyolxauhqui Imperative 2020," Dr. Machete, Liliana Conlisk Gallegos, medium: ink + color pencil + digital painting, 2019

The Gama of Invisibility

In a *CNN* investigation dated May 15, 2018, Bob Ortega found that the Border Patrol had not been properly tracking and recording deaths (as they are supposed to do since the late 1990s). They excluded fatalities reported by other law-enforcement agencies and neglected even deaths directly witnessed by agents. Over the 16 fiscal years ending on September 2017, *CNN* identified that at least 564 deaths were excluded from the Border Patrol's tally of 5,984. The actual number was closer to 6,548.

One of them was 18-year-old Darwin Cabrera, who in 2014 had survived the dangerous journey from Central America. Just as he crossed into El Paso, he was chased into one of the canals of the Rio Grande. Two days later, he was found face down in the water. "Even though the Border Patrol saw him go in and saw his body come out, his death did not count in their eyes. The agency's official tally of border-crossing deaths in their El Paso sector that year: Zero" (Ortega, 2018). To the binary mindset imbued in coloniality, there is a "right way" to cross, and those who do not follow it have forfeited their human value; they do not count.

The idea of not counting *es algo que se impone multidimensionalmente y por herencia*. It carries the mark of coloniality. The violence we see the Border Patrol enacting is parallel to the petty viciousness in quotidian and even "woke" manifestations. Many conscious and decolonial *transfronterizos* have unique ways of challenging and producing *conocimiento* which is devalued and not counted. From experience, the conscious *transfronterizo* knows, *que hay muchas cosas que pasan que según no cuentan*. I have personally experienced how my divergent proposals are misunderstood and berated. The persistent effect of coloniality possesses even those who say they love writers like Anzaldúa and label themselves as decolonialists.

It may be due to seeking validation within academic circles. Some *colegas* have deeply internalized that knowledge production is supposed to follow a certain pattern and they proudly embody *Gandalfesque* borders. This dissonance is showcased on social media comments on how some shall not pass when *they* are on patrol, implying that their expected formats and methodologies are a marker of academic superiority and sophistication. This is an internalization of the obsession with hierarchical thinking, homogeneity, and repetitive patterns. There are clear parallels of coloniality between border violence and the quotidian, petty violence like that one experienced by my mother when she went to a book presentation by a historian on the founding families of the city of Tijuana. She told the historian that our family had been around for generations before the supposed Spanish founding families, and he said, "*pero eran indios, los indios no cuentan.*"

This phenomenon of humans not counting, or *gente que no cuenta, no debe contar*, is a legacy of colonization and imperialism initially defined solely by racial difference. People migrate to the U.S. from places that "do not count" to the global north because their ways of life are devastated by greed and political turmoil brought on by mostly Western European and U.S. foreign policy and interventions (Prashad, 2020). In Latin America, this has included U.S. involvement in regime change, replacing popular politicians with corrupt sell-out dictators who allow free and open foreign investments and concessions to natural resources and land (Galeano, 1971; Chomsky, 2002; de Sousa Santos, 2006). The globalization of capitalism brought further devastation to laborers, the environment, and the overall economy of Latin American countries. In the border, especially in Tijuana, this materialized in the maquiladora industry (Funari & De la Torre, 2006).

Before leaving, migrants sell anything they have, objects with deep sentimental value. They physically leave the land, their loved ones, but they also begin an invisible displacement from the old self, who is often identified and understood as the whole self in its relation to the land. After this separation, you come to be in a dislocated, fragmented state and, in order to heal, Anzaldúa refers to the Coatlicue state: a process in which we re-visit the wound and where we make sense of "our greatest disappointments and painful experiences ... [which] can lead us to becoming more of who we are" (p. 46). It is painful to know. For the conscious *transfronteriza*, old wounds are confronted daily as new wounds are being inflicted. The trauma is reenacted over and over and confronted not only as a memory, but in its ever presence. The memory of a conscious *transfronteriza* is unique, formed by the time-loop of an eternal and intergenerational physical and spiritual groundhog-day, a limbo from which you find and share liberation by unearthing and exposing patterns that unite our *lucha*.

A Multidimensional *lucha*

Usually, when we talk about border trauma, it is directly related to overt acts of terrorism and violence inflicted on innocent people, the spilt blood of those who are NOT looking for a better life but are actually fighting in their own continent for the right to be and live, if only, survive in their ancestral lands. They are like gladiators forced into a coliseum, who literally fight for life to death. Many immigrants lose their lives on their way to the U.S. because they are being attacked from multiple fronts. The *coyotes*, or people who they pay thousands of dollars to guide them have been known to rape their clients, abandon them in the desert or in trains and trucks with tragic occurrences, which have included suffocation and dehydration. Cartels have also been known to attack migrants, selling them to organized crime, forcing them to smuggle drugs, harvesting their organs, enslaving them in U.S. American labor and sex markets. Others have been extorted, killed, and tortured in Mexico, thrown alive in acid tanks. This hell has many dimensions, and it extends beyond the desserts and the desolate spaces between the nations; it is also present at official border crossings.

Since 2004, the southern Arizona humanitarian organization *No More Deaths* has documented U.S. Border Patrol agents committing human rights abuses, ranging from cruel, unsafe, and unsanitary detention conditions to physical and sexual assault. In 2013, there was the case of 16-year-old Cruz Velazquez, a child who was coerced to cross the border with sodas laced with methamphetamines in his school backpack. The agents, knowing he had drugs, made him drink the liquid while they stood there laughing at him. He died. Add to this cases of the excessive force, overuse of electric stun guns, humiliation, and sexual harassment and molestation of people who simply want to cross the border and are submitted to such treatment with the sole reason of being suspect.

Sylvanna Falcon relates, in her essay "'National Security' and the Violation of Women: Militarized Border Rape at the US-Mexico Border": "The US-Mexico border represents an uneasy 'union' of the 1st and 3rd worlds. Due to disparaging levels of nation-state power, it is a contentious region that has been militarized to violently reinforce the territory of the US ... rape is routinely and systematically used by the state in militarization efforts at the US-Mexico border, and provoked by certain factors and dynamics in the region such as the influence of military culture on Border Patrol agents" (Falcon, 2016, p. 119). In these conditions, conscious *Transfronterizos* who can cross with papers but who still deal with other dimensions of this violence, emerge like luchadores. We cross the border daily and *la línea* is like a ring where we continuously enact the eternal battle. From the hyper-exposure we learn how to use the ropes to jump in and out, to push ourselves against them, to propel and comeback with even more momentum. Like *luchadores libres* say, this *lucha* is not fake; we also get hurt, very hurt and some of us also die from the long term and serious effects of the lesions.

We are fighting a multidimensional fight. Even when our plight may seem so different, we are all playing a unique role in this shift. We are after all, Nature. All dimensions of this fight share hidden roots that are continuously growing, mostly out of sight because we are made to not know. As the border, the in-between, itself expands and more are pushed into experiences of *frontera,* more will bear witness to the broad array of these patterns, which have always been blatantly there for the conscious *transfronterizo, que aprende a moverse bonito entre las esquinas de esta arena, cuadrilatero* of synchronized harmony and dissonance between the globalization of this hegemonic ideology and the intimacy of personal and ever so divergent experience.

∴

I was born in the U.S., but grew up thinking I was from Tijuana, because we lived in Tijuana and crossed the border daily to go to school. We had the luxury of a car, but many of my friends would cross by foot. It would take them hours to cross the border, and they had to stand there in the cold or in the heat. My mother was a naturalized citizen, but my father was not. He did not care to. He worked in Tijuana and his hard-earned pesos paid for all our expenses, including the extra set of taxes he paid the U.S. government because we were going to school there. As we waited at the border crossing my mother would always prompt us to hide our books. I remember the feeling of fullness in my chest, the numbness in my lips from the anxiety as I sat there waiting to be interrogated, to be looked at with suspicion and be treated, basically like shit. We hid the books under the seats so the agent would not have an excuse to ask more questions.

Sometimes they would send dogs out; they would come and sniff around us. I would pray the beasts would not make any weird gestures, or else, they would immediately think we were hiding something in our car. A fat border patrol agent wearing a suit two sizes too small would raise their black-leather-gloved hand in a forceful gesture demanding my mom to stop the car. Stop the car! And it always escalated quickly, STOP THE CAR GODDAMMIT!! The dogs would go around our car once, twice, three, four times. It was overkill.

I made sure my baby brother did not make a noise because what if that rose suspicion of ... who knows? Anything. I always made sure to never cry or show my fear, because, if I did, then they would think my parents were not my parents, or there would be another reason for my tears, were we hiding something? We never felt safe when crossing, my mom prepared us when we were on our way. Every single morning, *con ese miedo a los gringos*. We knew that if we made any remark, moved a bit too quick, or showed any signs of anything, that we could give them a reason and the RIGHT to humiliate us, to scrutinize us, berate us. We knew this because it happened many times before, and it happened many times after.

I lived in the fear of what they could do, as if my whole life and everything I ever knew could just end at their will. I clearly remember the shots of saliva from the corner of a border patrol agents mouth hit my mother's side window as he shouted at her to "go, go, go!" The dogs had nothing, again. Then they could say, "no hold on wait. Stop the car. Make them show us one of the birth certificates again." My heart would sink. "Ok, you can go now!" I was holding my breath. As I could feel the blood returning to the tips of my frozen fingers, as I lived it, I remembered it was not over. We would still need to pass the main booth. We knew it would happen again tomorrow, with another agent, maybe better, almost always worse. I knew it could always be worse. We did this every day. Sometimes twice a day, ever since I can remember.

On one occasion, when I was about nine years old, my aunt had a brand-new Cadillac. After a weekly Sunday dinner with the family in Tijuana, we headed back to San Ysidro. To cross the border, my uncle and my father went in one car, and my aunt, my mother and us children went in the Cadillac. When we got there, the border agent began asking my aunt many questions. Then he stopped asking and had us waiting in the car for a long period of time. The wait was torture. It was excruciating when you think the other person has all the power to decide what happens to you, especially when you know that to them, you do not count. It was justified because we did not look "American." After that long wait, we were sent to secondary inspection to wait at least another hour or so. Then suddenly an agent came to our car and asked my mother and aunt to step out.

At that point, they take us in. They pat my mom and aunt down, cuff them. We sit while they take my mom and aunt to a back room. Hours later they come out, my mother is in tears, gutted. They had made them strip down to their underwear in an act of utter humiliation. I am almost certain those pigs got off on that type of stuff. Then, they made us stand outside our car while we watched the dogs go inside and sniff it out. Of course, when we remember these stories, we have an array of anecdotes, one of the worse was my grandfather's experience. They stopped him and held him, they tortured him by giving him electric shocks because they wanted to force a false confession of drug possession from him. They finally let him go because it was not even true. He arrived at his home, not saying a word. The family found out years later that he had been greatly affected by this experience.

These low lives also attempted to humiliate our father figures countless of times in front of us. They spoke to my father with an air of supremacy, as if he was worthless. My father, the family hero, the same man who helped take his family out of poverty, the same man who has brought thousands of dollars into the U.S. in his lifetime, the same man who sacrificed his own needs to help me get through school, then college, the same man who would never hurt anyone, who would, in fact, take the shirt off his back to help anyone in need, even to those pieces of shit. They did that to my parents, the role models who represented all that I ever strived to become. Somehow, they were deserving of this treatment. What could I deserve? What was I worth?

While I was growing up, the rules for what was allowed and was not allowed into the border were not very clear to everyone crossing. We saw how countless perfectly fresh Mexican foods were disrespectfully and smugly thrown into the trash as officers laughed or made faces of disgust. More than once, I witnessed an agent hitting on my mother, asking inappropriate questions. When I grew older, I was also asked inappropriate questions by border agents. And they spoke to me with an air of intimidation, treating me like I was stupid, like they had the power to invent that I had something illegal in my car, all the while I presented my valid California ID, U.S. birth certificate, and U.S. Passport in a car with California license plates.

These kinds of experiences were so repetitive that I became a very anxious person with ZERO—and I mean ZERO—tolerance for bullshit. So many times, I drove home with angry tears in my eyes. I would think, "Damn, I should have told him, I should have said this, done that. I should have stood up for my parents." I was ashamed. Why was I such a coward? I felt so bad for them. My parents were and still are hardworking people. They are contributors to this American society. My mom was a volunteer at a public elementary school, where she worked all day for over 13-years and they never gave her a cent. My parents taught me to be giving and help others, especially those less fortunate. They told me to ignore people like the border agents, to stay away from trouble, that if I did that, it was going to be ok. This is but one example of how your agency can be almost taken away. Until, one day it becomes too much and liberation knocks at the door.

∴

One day something went off in me. I could no longer stand and watch these acts unfold without saying something, without at least trying. I started to fight back. On one of such occasions, I was dating an English guy, and he had an expired visa. I knew this because I coached him with the entire process. I told him to go ahead in line. He went and the border patrol agent said, welcome sir! He looked at his passport, did not even check the visa, and he let him pass. Then it was my brother's turn. The agent asked him for his passport and begins to look at it closely; he opens every single page, puts it through the machine, and begins interrogating my brother asking him how long he had been out of the U.S. and if he had brought anything with him. Then he makes him scan his fingertip. My blood is boiling. I shouted at the agent from the line, "hey how come you did not ask that white guy any questions? He has a foreign passport and yet you did not even look at his visa." He looked at me surprised, and he asked my brother if he knew me, "yeah she is my sister." And he goes, I did check his visa. And I said, "no, no you did not! You know how I know you didn't? Cause he is my boyfriend, and I know his visa is expired! Why are you treating my brother differently? He has a U.S. Passport!" My voice got louder and louder.

At that point, he asks for my passport. He looks at it and, as I keep asking him questions, he says, "move along, move along." I see that his colleagues begin reaching for their guns. And now you are gonna try to shoot me, GTFOH! On other occasions, I have had to step in for other people being mistreated by the agents. Every single time, my heart races like the first time. Crossing the border has never gotten easier for me. I don't know if it's because they are still horrible, or because I have some form of complex PTSD. But they keep doing things like this. One time, an elderly man only spoke Spanish. The agent was shouting at him, "do you understand? Hello!?! CAN YOU HEAR MEEEE?" I saw this, and from the other side of the room I said, "HEY, hey, hey, you! Stop it! Stop talking to that man in that way. Not speaking English is not a crime, and you know that, you need to serve people here with dignity and respect! Maam! Maam, nothing! Do your job RIGHT!"

I vowed to myself that whenever I witness such things, I will stand up for others. I do this every single time and especially for those who remind me of me before, intimidated and stripped of their power and agency. I tell myself "Do it for those who are killed due to this logic, for our ancestors, for every time your heart raced as a child, for the anger that ate your insides, and all the times you felt disgusted ... helpless." Something important happens when you no longer sit in silence, something as painful as it is liberating. You realize that the years of mistreatment, of fear and stress, of nervousness have all been a grave injustice, something unnecessary that should have never been.

From the recurring experience of having to be in flight or fight mode, I began to develop a keen sense for comebacks. I became a witty smart ass, unafraid of the consequences of breaking my silence. In my responses, in my attempts to defend my family's and my own right to be treated humanely while crossing the border, and even until this day in academia, I am seen as a disruptor, an unruly rebel, someone potentially dangerous.

This is why today; I react to bullshit with a quickness. I have experienced it too many times. I know the detrimental emotional and psychological consequences of allowing that to continue. I don't think twice, and people may read it as being emotional, but in fact, I am but attempting to nip at the bud the behaviors of coloniality in all their multidimensional shapes and forms. This is in fact our land, our ancestral land. And we are sharing it with everyone. How dare they say we do not belong. But, yet they do.

∶∶

I have ancestors who were born in Los Angeles, and they were "Mexicans" illegally thrown out of the U.S. White settlers who came from the East of the U.S. faked it until they forced themselves into rightful owners of the lands where my ancestors lived for thousands of years. They came and said that my family was less American than them because they were not white. They removed them illegally. My family were Indigenous, but it did not matter, because all Brown people were Mexicans to them. And we were the lucky ones. The thousands who refused to leave were lynched.

For us, for my family, like many other Chicanos and Latinos, we are simply home. For many years, this has been one of America's greatest kept secrets. Even though it is common knowledge, very few people know the history of the blood ties Latina/o/x's have to the entire American continent. The border crossed us is not a cliché. The border literally crossed us, when the settlers rounded us up and deported our ancestors illegally, when they imprisoned and lynched us to keep our ancestral lands and history hidden. It crossed us to live with intergenerational trauma, my great-great grandfather fought against the U.S. anarchist invasion of Baja California, my great grandfather fought as a nine-year-old in the Mexican Revolution next to Pancho Villa. He also had U.S. citizenship, and lived in the United States many years. He hated the way people were treated in the U.S. and he would stand up for people's rights. He would defend Japanese women who were exploited and sold as slaves. He knew a lot about homemade cures from fighting in the revolution, and helped many people who were dying of pneumonia in the U.S. He got in contact with the health services to provide a cure that he knew about; they ignored him and did not want it. This was the last straw for him. He was invalidated, and he saw others dehumanized. So he took his papers, tore them, and threw the pieces at the face of the last border patrol that ever interrogated him. José López Uribe, learn his name.

As a conscious *transfronteriza*, I grew up hearing these oral histories. I grew up living them in their revamped contemporary forms. Ask your family about yours, you might discover that a lot of the things you experience today are related to traumatic experiences your family has lived. Let your strengths tell the story of how you have endured. If you have no idea what I am talking about, pay more attention and listen to other perspectives. Maybe you disagree and think we are wrong or exaggerate about coloniality and its dire effects, but what if you are wrong? Can you live with the possibility that you could be the embodiment of borders?

References

Anzaldùa, G. (2012). *Borderlands: Las frontera: The new Mestiza* (4th ed.). Aunt Lute.

Chomsky, N. (2002). *Latin America, from colonization to globalization.* Ocean Press.

De Sousa Santos, B. (2006). *The rise of the global left.* AbeBooks.

Falcon, S. (2016). 'National security' and the violation of women: Militarized border rape at the US-Mexico border. In Women of Color Against Violence (Eds.), *Color of violence: The INCITE anthology.* INCITE!

Freire, P. (1970). *Pedagogy of the oppressed.* Bloomsbury.

Funari, V., & de la Torre, S. (2006). *Maquilapolis: City of factories* [Documentary].

Galeano, E. (1971). *Las venas abiertas de América Latina.* Monthly Review Press.

Iglesias Prieto, N. (2004). En pocas palabras: Representaciones discursivas de la frontera México-Estados Unidos. *Aztlan: A Journal of Chicano Studies, 29*(1), 145–153.

Mignolo, W. (2000). *Local histories/global designs: Coloniality, subaltern knowledges, and border thinking.* Princeton University Press.

Ortega, B. (2018, May 15). Border patrol failed to count hundreds of migrant deaths on US soil. *CNN.com.* https://www.cnn.com/2018/05/14/us/border-patrol-migrant-death-count-invs

Prashad, V. (2020). *Washington bullets: A history of the CIA, coups, and assassinations.* Monthly Review Press.

World Migration Report 2020. (2019). United Nations International Organization for Migration. https://www.un.org/sites/un2.un.org/files/wmr_2020.pdf

CHAPTER 2

Field Notes from the Borderlands
Reflections on Reading, Writing, and Travel

Santiago Vaquera-Vásquez

This Is a Shout Out

To those who listen to our stories.
To those who are no longer with us, but who live on.
To those trapped in the borderlines between nations.
To those who live and work in countries where forgetting is reigning
supreme:
> forgetting communities that helped shape it, so that the
> country can move forward,
> forgetting its academics who help in the construction of its
> knowledge
> forgetting its intellectuals who have every right to champion
> the nation that they believe in and
>> also speak up when that nation forgets.

To those who have every right to question and resist authoritarianism
and dogma.
This is a shout out to them.
To the workers in our cities and towns, who work in the streets, make
our cities splendid, and keep our
> movement flowing.

To the many arrested around the world for speaking up and asking to be
recognized for their ethnicity, their
> religion, their sexuality.

To those who, as they discover that traditional forms of resistance are
being cut back, find new ways to
> resist, to speak up.

This is a shout out to them.
To my Latino/a /x community, the 50 millions of us living, working, and
contributing to the United States,
> demanding to not be sent back to live in the shadows.

To those who cross borders because *we have choices*. We cross because
we need to resist those who would
> try to silence us, support those who have been silenced, and
> *luchar* for those who have been caged
> by a border machine.

To those who resist marginalization.
To those students who sit in our classes and help us remain honest in
this dialogue that is learning—they
> learn from us, we learn from them.

To those who create art in their everyday being.
This is a shout out to them.
This is a shout out for us, the urgent voices who fight to keep our stories
alive.

The Story of My Border

I often say that I was a born a Mexican in the United States. My parents crossed
the border a few months before I was born. Hecho en México, born in the USA,
I also say. My childhood was spent crossing borders, from the US/Mexico border
whenever I went to visit my *abuelos* and *parientes* in Mexicali, to the linguistic
borders as I switched between *inglés* and Spanish. Growing up in a small farming
community in northern California, as I did, I spent a lot of time in the company
of the sizable Mexicano community there. We were all products of migration,
some came before—my grandfather first visited that part of California in the
1940's as a Bracero—others later, often pulled by family that had settled there.

English came into my life when I started school: I became a Mexican
American. My summers were spent in Mexicali, and my school year was spent
in Northern California. Crossing borders was all my siblings and I knew. In
my teens, my life was further upended when my parents got divorced and my
sister, two years younger than me, had her leg amputated because of cancer.
With the divorce and my sister in the hospital, my mother had to separate her
children. My youngest sister went to live with my grandmother in Mexicali,
my other sister and my brother went with my father, and my mom moved to
Mountain View to be near my sister, who was undergoing chemotherapy at
Stanford. As the oldest, I was left with no home. I was considered weird within
my larger extended family: talkative as a child, I grew more silent and awkward
as a teen. My escape was books and music. The only apartment mom could
find within her budget did not allow children. Ironically, it was right across
the street from a junior high that I attended for one semester. That was when I

started trying to become invisible. In the mornings, I would sneak down to the parking lot and cross the street to go to school. In the afternoons, I would have to stay out of sight as I made my way back to the apartment. The rest of the day, I would have to be as quiet as possible until mom came home from work. After a few months of this, and a few close calls where the apartment manager almost caught me, mom was able to convince one of her sisters to take me in. I was moved to Imperial Beach, California. Right on the border.

Whenever I could, I would stay in the hospital with my sister. The nurses set up a cot by her bed. I would tell her stories, crack jokes, plan adventures with her. We tried to pretend that we were not in a hospital surrounded by dying children.

But sometimes.

It was too much.

At times I would wake up in the middle of the night to the sounds of various medical devices working hard to keep kids alive. In those times when I was in the hospital with my sister, we were living in an in-between, liminal, space. We were stuck between borders in a strange, almost science fiction world. It was hard at times, but there were other moments when we were able to pull out some sort of joy amongst all the sadness. That was then I began listening to the stories around me.

Remembering it now, I realize it was all preparation for my own wandering life, my own journeys as a border crosser. And though I didn't know it at the time, I was growing into myself as a person who prefers to be in the in-between; a person who finds comfort in the middle world. Wandering is the story of my border.

What follows is a report on border crossing: field notes, photos, passport stamps from living in and on borderlines. This is a story about forms of departure that are also forms of arrival. They are reflections on a life of reading, writing, and traveling across borders. For this selection, they are centered on three cities that have been important stops in my border crossing journey: Tijuana, Madrid, and Istanbul.

Tijuana: Names on the Wall

Here is a photo. July, 1999. Tijuana. The photo is of the border wall on the beach. On the wall, a local activist organization has placed large plywood sheets, painted white. On them are the names, ages, and places of origins of everyone who has died while trying to cross the border since the institution of Operation Gatekeeper in October 1994. There are hundreds of names.

I took this photo during a visit to Tijuana to visit a friend. One afternoon we walked down to the beach where we saw the names on the wall. We walked along the wall in silence, reading the names. I was struck by the number of children who had died.

Years earlier, after my mother was able to reunite her kids under one house in Imperial Beach, we lived in an apartment on the edge of Border Field State Park, a large coastal wetlands area that bordered the city right up to the border wall. At night, my siblings and I would watch TV, while Border Patrol helicopter searchlights crisscrossed our apartment complex, looking for people who had crossed at the beach. One night, my mother heard noises in the back and went outside to investigate. She found two brothers hiding from the *migra*. Rather than tell them to leave, she invited them inside and said they could sleep in the living room. The older brother had a family in the central valley and had gone back to Mexico to bring his younger brother across. My mother listened to their story and offered to drive them. We still had family up in northern California, and she had been wanting to visit her brothers. After a couple of days of putting things in order, we all got in the car and drove up north with the brothers. For my mother, it was all about reuniting as family. Family is important for her and the maintenance of those bonds was paramount.

The border names on the wall did not last very long. When I returned to Tijuana, months later, the panels were gone. But since then, every time I go back to the beach to see the wall, I think of the names, of the people who had tried to cross but had been caught in the borderline. I also think of those who made it across, like those brothers we once helped in the early 1980's. We never saw them again, but their story remains in the border crossing stories told by my family.

Madrid: Chicano Carrying in His Coat Pocket a Passport

A passport, as Salman Rushdie once noted, is a book. But what is that story? In many ways, it is an autobiography written in entry and exit stamps: each stamp is a chapter. The story of my passport is one of frequent travel. I am currently on my fourth passport. My third one had to be renewed six months early, when I was living in Turkey. I had already run out of room for stamps, despite the fact that three years earlier I had gone to the US embassy in Mexico City to have pages added. By 2017, when I had to renew my passport, it was filled with stamps from Spain, France, England, Oman, Turkey, Ecuador, Colombia, and Mexico. There were stamps upon stamps, marking out years of constant travel. When I read any of my passports, I see: conversations with students in Muscat, Oman while walking around the *souq*; saying goodbye to my friends in a bar in

Madrid at two in the morning; going home to pack a bag and be at the airport by 4 am for a flight to Istanbul; arriving to Paris to meet my sister in a café and then the two of us heading to the Gare du Nord to take a train to Amsterdam; walking around downtown Mexico City with a friend talking about our favorite books and movies; being driven in an over-stuffed taxi across Izmir, Turkey, in one night to a soundtrack of arabesque music.

For me, my passport's story is largely happy: memories of travel, conversations, and exchange. But for customs officials it often tells a very different story. Standing in line at passport control in Madrid in late 2005, I watched as the passport agent flipped slowly through my book, looking for an empty spot where he could place the exit stamp. Finally, he returned it to me, looked me in the eye and said: *Usted. Viaja. Mucho.* You. Travel. A lot.

To the customs official, my passport was not a happy one. All he saw were filled pages of entry and exit stamps, and three years left before the passport expired. For him, my passport told a story of instability, of rootlessness: in a sense, it was the story of a migrant's shame.

If it had been possible, I would have had a conversation with the customs official. I would have pointed out how each entry and exit stamp marked a part of a larger story. Not of shame, but of connection, of communion. Here is one: three friends, all immigrants, walking around central Madrid on a summer day. One is a Chicano, a member of the Mexican diaspora, living at the time between Spain and the US, and the other two are Peruvian, living in Madrid. The three are talking about Mexican popular culture, in particular, the impact of Luis Miguel in Latin America. Suddenly, the two Peruvians break into a *Luismi* pose, one leg bent back, head bent down, a hand almost touching the forehead. For them, this is his classic pose, a stance almost of defiance. The Chicano snaps a photo of the two friends, performing *Luismi* in the middle of a narrow street in central Madrid.

Istanbul: *Yabancı—Extranjero*

On a flight from Munich to Istanbul, I sat near an older Turkish gentleman. He kept trying to talk to me in Turkish. By then, I had been traveling back and forth between the United States and Turkey for more than a decade, and I had picked up enough of the language to be able to say that I couldn't speak Turkish. The man didn't believe me. He would ask me a question, I would respond that I couldn't speak, and he would turn to others in the rows around us and start talking to them, pointing me out. I imagined he couldn't believe that I was a *yabancı*, a foreigner. I would say, *"ben yabancı"* (I am foreign) and he would exclaim that I looked Turkish. I told him I was Mexican—"*ben meksikalıyım*"—and he pointed out that my Turkish was very good. Then he continued to talk to others around us. I imagined that he was telling them that I was a sad case, a Turk who had not learned to speak Turkish, and so I pretended to be Mexican. Perhaps he considered that I was one of those German-Turks, *Alamancı,* who had lost their mother tongue. I don't know how, but I finally convinced him that I was neither Turkish nor *Alamancı.* He told me he lived in Germany and was working for the airline. He was flying home to see family. I told him I was going to visit friends in Istanbul. Though I didn't tell him, I felt we were in some ways similar: we were living the consequences of migration. As I sat back in my seat, ready to fall asleep on the flight to Turkey, the man reached over and gifted me an airline sleeping mask.

More than "foreigner" *yabancı* literally means "stranger." And having lived most of my life in a country that has often wanted to treat us as foreigners or strangers in our own land, I liked being able to self-identify in Turkey as one. *Ben yabancı.*

We Are the Sum of Our Connections

I grew up in a family of storytellers. When I was young, my summers were spent in Mexico, in Mexicali, right across the border from California. In the evenings, I remember my uncles and aunts sitting around the kitchen table telling stories, about relatives, about people they knew, and sometimes, they would tell ghost stories. These were the ones that chilled my spine, even to this day. Mexicali seemed to be full of these stories.

But more than types of stories, it was the act of storytelling that got me. Because it is in stories that we start constructing community, we start knitting together and giving shape to our lives. Inevitably, among these stories, there was one about the friend, the relative, the cousin, the uncle who crossed the border and left, the aunt who disappeared, the sister, who died: the one who went away. And in the telling of their stories, they were bringing back that person, tying that person back into the present through a thread of history and storytelling.

This is why we tell stories. We bear witness, we bring back those who are ours, we weave our community together. Storytelling is a form of weaving one to another. We recover the stories of those we lost so that we can continue to add meaning to that person, that place, that community.

Mine is a community bound by story and travel, threaded across distance, held together by history, and bound in a book that travels with me. Part of my job—probably the smallest part—is to tell a story, the other half is to listen to others tell me theirs. In this way, hopefully, we can bridge those things that would attempt to separate us.

If there is one constant in my life, it is crossing borders. If my work has any meaning, it's because I live/travel across borders without fear nor with a fixed route—wandering is my friend—it's because I often carry a soundtrack—in my head—it's because the people I meet always have interesting stories to tell. While others fear border crossing because of the supposed danger, I prefer it for the cultures and dialogues that arise in the meeting of communities: yes, I am an unrepentant border crosser.

Dedication: This One Is for You

I was born a Mexican in the United States, then I became a Mexican-American when I learned English. It was in college that I became a Chicano. Entering the university in 1984 was momentous. Not just because I was the first member of my family to go to college, but because I began to shed my invisibility cape that I had constructed for myself. Becoming a college radio DJ at a punk rock radio station was one of my first steps. New DJ's at the station always started on an overnight slot, two to six am, so that they could develop their skills. I found my voice there, telling stories about the bands and the music as I constructed on the soundtrack of my life. After that semester, when I was asked what slot I would like, I decided to go with the time slot before my show, ten to two AM Saturday nights. That slot became mine for the next four years, before I left for Mexico City for a year. When I returned, I took up a Friday morning slot, because I had been offered a program on Rock en Español at the other campus station. That slot was Saturday night. It was a rough beginning, as the listening audience was made up of mainly families working in the orchards or on the farms. Their musical tastes leaned towards *norteño* or *onda grupera*. They wanted Los Tigres del Norte, I gave them Soda Stereo. They wanted Rocío Durcal, I gave them Alaska y Dinarama.

If I were to go back the radio, I would give them Café Tacvba, El Gran Silencio, Las Cafeteras, Radio Futura, and La Maldita Vecindad: *bandas* who crossed musical and linguistic borders. *Bandas* who sing songs about migration and border crossing.

I would turn on the microphone and say: "I'm going to play you all a song. One about people like you and me. One about border crossers. One about communities that in the face of adversity continue to endure, that resist being silenced, forgotten, or forced into the shadows."

One for all of us. One that is going to be a shout out.

We resist, we persist, we continue.

We have to continue. To remind those who would deny us our presence, that some of us did not cross the border, the border crossed us. We have to continue fighting for our stories. To stop would be to allow ourselves to accept marginalization, our "excuse me" tongues, and the feeling that we are not good enough. That we just do not belong.

And yet we do.

So, let's listen to this song, this dedication that I have for you, and then, let's sing it together.

CHAPTER 3

The Playas de Tijuana Mural Project
Digital Storytelling, Portraiture and U.S.-Mexico Border Art

Lizbeth De La Cruz Santana

My formation in Latin American testimonial literature, community-engaged scholarship, and digital storytelling has shaped much of the work that I currently do that documents the stories of migrants who entered the United States as minors ("childhood arrivals") and remained with a non-citizen status. Fieldwork in Tijuana, Guadalajara, and California have inspired the creation of a community mural that aims to bring to public attention the United States childhood arrivals dilemma.

The Playas de Tijuana Mural Project[1] is located on the western point of the U.S.-Mexico border separating San Diego from Playas de Tijuana. It's the first art piece visitors can see when approaching the beach. Its symbolic location interpolates outsiders to engage the mural both as a memorial and a critique to the intersection between U.S. criminal and immigration law that makes deportable all non-citizen migrants.

Before the global pandemic, there was a visible contrast of both sides of the border, where the Mexican side had constant visitors, music—it was alive. Visitors could get near the border and touch the fence. As this is one of the most visited spaces of the wall, the mural project has helped begin a conversation on who is vulnerable to deportation in the U.S. Its visible placement and magnitude of the portraits makes visitors acknowledge the mural, which alludes to the stories and faces of those marked by deportation who exist and should not be ignored.

U.S.-Mexico Border Art

When the 2016 election results were announced, I found myself traveling to Playas de Tijuana. The Humanizing Deportation project[2] team traveled to Mexico for a week-long training on digital storytelling at el Colegio de la Frontera Norte (COLEF). As part of our practice, we visited various symbolic sites along the border. I grew up crossing the border on our way to Guadalajara, Jalisco and experienced border enforcement complexities. These have shaped much of my interrogations as a Ph.D. candidate. As an adult and coming into

© LIZBETH DE LA CRUZ SANTANA, 2022 | DOI:10.1163/9789004521155_004

FIGURE 3.1   *The Playas de Tijuana Mural Project*

this location as a researcher, the questions and reflections that arose have formed the basis of the *Playas de Tijuana Mural Project*.

After concluding our first day of training, the research team was taken to Friendship Park in Playas de Tijuana. There, it was impossible to miss the art painted on the border fence. There were many images and messages painted, yet the message was up to the visitor to decipher. There was no description to guide those who found themselves here for the first time. Luckily for us, Guillermo Alfonso Meneses, professor at el COLEF accompanied us and shared as much information as he could. I compared this space to the Otay border point, where you can see crosses honoring migrants who have died attempting to cross the border. Besides reading articles on this space in Otay, our taxi driver educated us on the importance of this installation and the history of how the wall was constructed. Those who painted here took back this wall—reclaimed this space and transformed a wall connected to violence, death, human rights violations, and the attempt to prevent migration and enable the expulsion of an undesired immigrant.

One of the murals that impacted me the most was the veterans in distress mural that includes the upside-down American flag and the names of some of the U.S. veterans who have faced deportation from the country they took an oath to defend. I questioned, how can a military veteran who fought at war or conflict be deported? Something is wrong with using deportation as a punitive punishment—especially for this population.

Digital Storytelling

In 2017 as part of the Humanizing Deportation team, I spent my summer in Tijuana. The foreign spaces I would read about in order to familiarize myself with the border separating Tijuana and San Diego now had a more vivid memory. There I continued to document the border wall art and was left with two images that read "let us cross" and "ten years." The first image made sense to me, given the context. Yet the second was given meaning through the voices of the people who shared with us their stories and experiences with deportation. Through our community narrators, I learned that ten years indicated their punishment, their "castigo" after being exiled from the country most perceived as their home and where their family, culture, and life connections remain.

That summer became crucial in understanding the experiences of a community of immigrants that were somewhat forgotten from the immigrant's rights movement within the United States, media, and academic scholarship. Their authored digital narratives for the Humanizing Deportation project allowed for not only the research team to become familiar with the myriad of elements that triggered their deportation but also to document life after expulsion as experienced and communicated by them. As my advisor Robert McKee Irwin shares in many of the project's public presentations, "community storytellers are the knowledge creators."

The narrative aspect of digital storytelling has created a narrative path that gives life to abstract art and spaces—such as the ones found at the border. There is some danger in trusting people to enter particular areas and expecting them to have a meaningful encounter with the contents that are there or to walk away with the message intended. For this specific context, we can expect people to come in with prior knowledge and might not require the creators of the art to explain it to them—yet for me, presenting art without narrative fails to create impactful consciousness and action-driven participatory change.

In the hopes to eliminate the possibility that people may not understand what they are looking at the border in an intended manner, the *Playas de Tijuana Mural Project* facilitates educating visitors about deportation through the stories of people who have been impacted by displacement. In this sense, the mural project engages in narrative work and connects the dots through art and digital humanities.

The Humanizing Deportation archive hosts many stories tied to deportation drawn to conceptualize and theorize on migrant knowledge that often remains silent or forgotten. From these, my research centers on the stories told by childhood arrivals. This population is widely known as the DACA recipients and the dreamers. Yet, as my research suggests, this definition is limiting and excludes many others. Specifically those who have been previously deported before the implementation of the Deferred Action for Childhood Arrivals DACA program and those whose DACA eligibility criteria exclude. These observations led me to question who counts as a childhood arrival, revealing the real childhood arrivals through the mural project.

Artivism

As a researcher and someone connected with the community I am collaborating with, I questioned the limits of my engagement as a university student. I often found myself dealing with the guilt of listening and knowing the stories of those who have confided in us. Many considered our work as something innovative and admirable. Yet, I felt that I was not doing enough and that merely hosting stories in an archive was not reaching its full potential. Often, in public presentations, attendees would ask the team what other forms of engagement we were pursuing besides documenting. And repeatedly, stating that the project aimed to create stories did not feel enough. Considering these circumstances and feelings of guilt, I decided to find resources in the university to help solve this in some capacity. Although I value the process of creating stories with the community, for it has allowed me to make public knowledge on deportation, I sought to challenge the research component and to engage in reciprocity. To give back to the community we were collaborating with.

The UC Davis Mellon Public Scholars 2019 fellowship became the support I was seeking. The fellowship helped clear some of the issues I was navigating, and it allowed for a creative project of this kind to come to fruition. I worked alongside Mauro Carrera, lead artist of the project, Enrique Chui, who facilitated the space at the border, and professor and artist Maceo Montoya, who became my faculty advisor for the project.

In 2016 after seeing all the art at the border, my intention to have a mural on the border point by the beach related to the work we were doing in the Humanizing Deportation project manifested. After three years of fieldwork in Tijuana, and now with the fellowship's support, a mural that would engage the community we collaborated with became a possibility.

I had known Mauro Carrera from other events in Fresno, CA, and I mentioned the idea of creating a mural in Tijuana early on in my academic journey at Davis. We just needed funding. And that funding came through. This fellowship offered a generous stipend, which helped cover the cost of painting materials, meals for the entire team, and travel costs. It became seed money for a project that continues to outlive its intended working period due to public interest and the community's desire to continue the work we began.

Selection of Storytellers

I selected the stories that would be highlighted on the mural by listening to the Humanizing Deportation archive and considered my relationship with several of the storytellers who had faced deportation, who lived in Tijuana, and others who held DACA status and lived in the U.S.

In every step that took place to make this project possible, working through an ethical practice was crucial and has supported the success of the project. Therefore, I wanted to make sure I knew their stories best as possible and had their trust in engaging in a project of this magnitude.

The storytellers selected to be a part of the mural project are deported veteran Andy de León, Dreamer mom Montserrat Godoy, Dreamer mom and proto dreamer profile Tania Mendoza, Isaac Rivera, who falls within the dreamer profile, then DACA recipient Karla Estrada, DACA recipient Jairo Lozano, and John Gúzman. John was deported in his teen years but was able to appeal his deportation and now holds U.S. permanent resident status.

Portraiture

For the public not familiar with the mural, there are seven large grayscale portraits painted on the border fence. The portraits were painted in the historic Casa del Túnel in Tijuana. Painter Enrique Chui facilitated the space. In our nine days in the studio, many of the migrants portrayed on the mural, community storytellers for the Humanizing Deportation project, as well as allies all accompanied lead artist Mauro Carrera and myself in the painting of the portraits. The fact that the

The video accompanying this figure is freely available online at https://doi.org/10.6084/m9.figshare.20472507

FIGURE 3.2   Andy de León

The videos accompanying this figure are freely available online at https://doi.org/10.6084/m9.figshare.20472774 https://doi.org/10.6084/m9.figshare.20472786 https://doi.org/10.6084/m9.figshare.20472801

FIGURE 3.3   Issac Rivera

The video accompanying this figure is freely available online at https://doi.org/10.6084/m9.figshare.20472819

FIGURE 3.4   Jairo Lozano

The videos accompanying this figure are freely available online at
https://doi.org/10.6084/m9.figshare.20472840
https://doi.org/10.6084/m9.figshare.20472954

FIGURE 3.5   Karla Estrada

The videos accompanying this figure is freely available online at
https://doi.org/10.6084/m9.figshare.20472966
https://doi.org/10.6084/m9.figshare.20730811

FIGURE 3.6   Monseratt Godoy

The videos accompanying this figure is freely available online at https://doi.org/10.6084/ m9.figshare.20472984 https://doi.org/10.6084/ m9.figshare.20730835

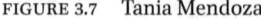

FIGURE 3.7   Tania Mendoza

migrants represented in the mural were painting their pictures and supported every step of the mural made this project unique and memorable. This method allowed the participants to become artists themselves and specifically for story-tellers to continue authoring their own stories and self-representation materials. This was a critical aspect of the project. I did not want an artist to simply come to the border and paint the stories of interest, but rather to facilitate once again the tools for the community to continue telling their stories. As unofficial painters, we became *rascuache* artists, utilizing the tools we had to make this work—this time not only with the digital stories but also through their artistic creation.

As the border fence is not a traditional wall in which murals are painted on, the portraits were installed on the fragmented bars that make up the fence. After the images were done, we cut them into strips to position them on the border fence. We worked from the eyes outward to make sure we did not lose the essence of the image. In a way, this interrupted and disjointed surface allowed us to send additional messages. The portraits can be best seen depend-ing on where the viewer is standing, and the images are disrupted because these are complex and multifaceted stories.

The elusive and profound faces that replicate a greyscale photograph invite the public to inquire on who is painted there and why. During painting and installation sessions, this was the most frequent question we would receive from visitors who would approach the team. To provide answers when the team was not on-site to explain the project's mission, the use of Quick Response

(QR) codes attempted to provide access to some of the dimensions and textures of the stories shared.

Art and Technology

The innovative aspect of the QR codes called the attention of national and international news media. When scanned, these direct audiences to the narratives of the storytellers hosted on YouTube. The QR codes are placed all around the wall and made available on the project's website, along with downloadable educational materials.[3]

As mentioned before, my desire to have a way in which visitors at the border point could have guidance in what they were seeing was crucial in this project. The implementation of the QR codes became the answer. Once visitors scan the codes with their phone, they are directed to YouTube, and the narrative selected starts to play. After listening to the story, they can then make a choice to share it with their networks. In this way, not only are they listening to the stories but can also engage beyond that and help bring awareness to the issue. As this is one of the most visited spaces at the border, I hope that the mural's storytellers can get legal help. For me, their cases are simple, they just need the right support, and I know that exists.

FIGURE 3.8   *The Playas de Tijuana Mural Project*

The Longevity of the Mural during COVID-19

The mural represents the illegalization of a population of migrants that hold strong and even exclusive ties to the U.S. It centers the voice of those who are not represented in the national conversation around immigration issues. The mural and all its components then invite audiences to listen, to do their research, and engage in action.

Although the materials used to create the mural were intended to last for more than five years, unfortunately, due to the current global pandemic, the timeline for preserving the mural indicates that it will eventually start to fade. I do not see this as an adverse effect but more as a symbolic erasure and silence of the deportation of childhood arrivals in academic, political, and social movement practices. The erasure of the stories also communicates the fading of their stories beyond the boundaries of the border and take us to consider the invisibility surrounding the experiences of childhood arrivals in the U.S. and once returned to their country of birth. What is essential here is to remember that the mural was there, that it existed, and that the stories told to create it are still present and accessible.

In sum, through the mural, my intention is for the public not only to consider the stories of DACA recipients and the dreamers like Karla and Jairo but also to understand that the way our immigration and criminal justice system works allows for military veterans such as Andy de León to be deported. Although he had permanent resident status, he was still deportable. I want people to understand that deportation not only affects the person who is being displaced, but that it also has an enduring effect on their children. Such is the case of Montserrat and Tania. Deportation, in their cases, complicates their roles as mothers and often denies their motherhood.

I also want people to understand that before the original DACA version was instituted in 2012, other dreamers were previously deported. This type of relief or any other relief introduced has yet to include those who have been deported but still meet all the eligibility criteria versions of the Dream Act and other proposals introduced. I seek to inform that childhood arrivals are not merely defined by their immigration status or lack of status, but that they deserve a life with dignity and equal opportunities to their counterpart U.S. citizen neighbors, friends, and family. Additionally, I want people to consider that not everyone that gets deported has a criminal record. Our institutions and society criminalize some migrants. But even those childhood arrivals who hold a criminal record should be given the opportunity and pathways to make up for their actions.

FIGURE 3.9   *The Playas de Tijuana Mural Project*

In my doctoral dissertation, I suggest that the receiving country, in this case, Mexico, should implement useful programs to facilitate their incorporation and to consider the hardships in assimilating to a country foreign to them. For this reason, the mural was painted on the Mexican part of the border, as this issue not only pertains to the U.S. but to the Mexican state as well. Regarding the U.S., I plead for eliminating deportation as a punitive punishment for all childhood arrivals and for policies on this population to consider also those deported and who have self-repatriated.

FIGURE 3.10   Humanizing Deportation Project

Notes

1 https://lizbethdelacruzsantana.com/about
2 http://humanizandoladeportacion.ucdavis.edu
3 https://lizbethdelacruzsantana.com/the-faces-behind-the-mural

CHAPTER 4

Life on the U.S.-Mexico Border, 1970–1980

Víctor M. Macías-González

Growing up along the U.S.-Mexico border was complicated. Most people assume the border is an area of poverty and deprivation. As a contact zone, it is a region of complex hybridity, and surprising cosmopolitanism. Those who grew up there, with two nationalities and economic privilege, experienced a relatively porous international boundary where they had the best of both worlds. In my border childhood, although I did not know it then, I witnessed the demise of an old world, a world typical of the 1920s to the 1970s, when a small binational elite lived, studied, worked, and shopped on both sides of the border with relative ease. You could walk over the three bridges spanning the river, or ride a tram, or drive your car, and within minutes, you were in another country. The distance was minimal. I cross more space driving from La Crescent, Minnesota into La Crosse, Wisconsin, over the Mississippi River, than across the Río Grande from Ciudad Juárez, Chihuahua, into El Paso, Texas. That world is long gone, the victim of drug wars, the 9–11 Terrorist attacks, and the Central American refugee crisis. To cross into the U.S. now, one experiences a hyper militarized border, where x-ray machines see through your car, one is assumed suspect, and border guards clad in kevlar interrogate you using what they learned during a 90-day training. They ask you "the purpose of your visit to Mexico," based on your demeanor and responses, they decide whether you and your vehicle need to be searched and inspected further. It is an upsetting and stressful experience that may easily become a two hour wait in queue, or longer, and may include a strip search. I imagine the impositions on our freedom of movement were not much different from those the Israelis have imposed on Palestinians. In my childhood, crossing the border checkpoints was at most a 40-minute ordeal, usually less, as you sat in your car and waited for 20 to 40 cars ahead of you to proceed through the check point, taking no longer than it takes for you to get through the booth at an airport car rental. Now, there are anxious, nervous border guards who are as stressed as their tired, aggressive canines, and surveillance cameras with sophisticated biometric software. To be truthful, one can bypass using an expedited clearance crossing system like Sentri; you pay some $125 per person for a five-year permit and thanks to Neoliberalism, escape the Orwellian border crossing experience. The international boundary's trauma was less in my childhood in the 1970s, as the following vignettes show.

I was born in El Paso, Texas in 1970, but I grew up in Ciudad Juárez, Chihuahua. I was aware of being an American that lived in Mexico from a young age, a dual-nationality anchor baby of sorts. Every few years my parents would get us dressed up for an appointment at the U.S. consulate to register as an expatriate. A woman consular clerk seemed to always handle our paperwork. I enjoyed hearing the alien sounds of English—grunk, threeh, shrak, wuh, a harsh guttural cacophony--and looking at the pale faces of the staff. They looked and sounded like the Americans on television; they did not have the twangs of Texan Anglos. The woman who processed our paperwork made a big production of my hair ("what lovely curls!") and struggled to ascertain my hair color, holding it up to a printed card that had labeled color swatches ("no, it's not black, it's dark brown"). She also dealt with my double-barreled last name, which I signed on my photograph despite the Texan birth certificate that only listed my father's last name. I must have been in the first grade the first time we went. When the clerk shook her head at my use of my second last name—my mother's last name—I replied, "At school, my teacher taught me to use both of my last names." And she would fret, check with a supervisor, and let it go, as my mother said, "He is the oldest and has to have both of our names, you know how the Texans are, they only let their Mexicans use one last name." The clerk noted "the name on the form has to match name on the birth certificate, it is okay if the signature on the photograph differs." So, early on, I learned that on one side of the border I had one name—Macias, without an accent—but on the other, I had two, *Macías González*, with accents. I also learned a more valuable lesson: with tact and determination, you can question a bureaucrat.

The document we received from the consulate allowed us to cross the U.S.-Mexico border easily. Waving it and saying "American citizen," I could quickly get through the border guard station at the International Bridge. Since my mother did not learn to drive until the early 1980s, it meant that throughout the 1970s, we crossed the border regularly aboard the international tram or bus. This mode of transport wound through the central districts of both cities and had its own dedicated lane on the downtown bridges: the Santa Fe Bridge had one-way traffic from Mexico into the U.S., and the Stanton Street Bridge had one-way traffic from the U.S. to Mexico. We took the tram on by the old Federal Customshouse in Juárez, zoom up the Avenida Juárez—clogged with bars and curio shops that catered to American tourists and GIs out for a good time— and we would alight from the tram, flash our cards, and get back on the tram at the American checkpoint, on El Paso Street on the American side. Then, the tram would proceed north, passing rapidly through the retail district in El Paso where Mexican shoppers thronged looking for bargains. We would get dropped off in downtown El Paso, some eight blocks north of the border station, and headed for the nicer shops. Thom McAn's for shoes and belts, Lerner's Dress shop for my mother's outfits, The Popular Dry Goods Department Store for cologne or ties for my father, and JC Penney's for my clothes. The stores were always bright and the ambient music, together with the chill of refrigerated air conditioning, made shopping a delightful, almost sensual experience. Sometimes we would go to the lunch counter at the Kress store—I loved the hot dogs and the popcorn there, in front of San Jacinto Plaza. We might browse at Woolworth's or Newberry's—discount retailers that did not use refrigerated air conditioning but offered bargain finds. The poor shopped there. I liked to look at the cheap Japanese toys there, although, truth be told, I preferred Toys by Roy, at Basset Center, which sold the most beautiful British and Belgian hand painted and mechanical toys.

Before hopping back on the tram, we might visit my sister Gloria's podiatrist to order a new pair of shoes for her (she had flat feet), and at the end of the day, we would stop at Silva's supermarket to pick up groceries. On those occasions my sister's stroller did double duty as a grocery cart, although on these short, quick tram trips, we would not buy more than a small bag of groceries—Hershey's Instant chocolate milk, baby formula, bacon, pancake mix, Treetop apple juice, cream cheese, or La Choy soy sauce. These were things that we were running low on or that my mom needed for a new recipe and could not wait until Dad would go and pick up larger grocery trips in the car, usually at night, after traffic on the bridges lessened. Late in the evenings, the migrant farmworkers congregated along the streets of South El Paso. They spent the night there, waiting for the farmers' trucks to come in to pick them up at 4 AM so they would arrive at their workplaces up and down the Rio Grande Valley at 5:30 AM. It was entire families, sleeping on cardboard boxes, with their belongings in grocery bags and farm tools in tow. I asked "are they gypsies?" and my father laughed. "They are workers, and if they go home to rest, someone else will take their job away, so they wait here, to be hired in the morning."

On these evening or night car trips across the border, we ranged further into El Paso, to the bigger grocery stores like Fedmart or Safeway. I asked dad to stop at the mall, Bassett Center, or we would stop for ice cream at Baskin Robbins. My father loved the taste of American milk, butter, cream cheese, maple syrup, and Grape Nuts cereal—his father, *don* Carlos, had grown up in Detroit, Michigan in the 1920s and 1930s, at the end of the Revolution. Don Carlos had a taste for American food, especially American breakfasts—and holiday food. He introduced his children to pumpkin and apple pies, egg nog, fruit cake, fried chicken, and roast beef. To accompany all this food, there were condiments that were not yet common in most Mexican homes: different types of mustards and mayonnaises, ketchup, Worcestershire sauce, horseradish sauce, Louisiana hot sauce, orange marmalade, and blue cheese dressing. I took my milk cold, with Hershey's Instant Chocolate milk mix. It came in a yellow tin with an illustrated history of chocolate in the back. It is not sold anymore. Unlike the Mexican knock offs, like Carlos V, it dissolved easily into the cold milk, without heat.

These things, that I took for granted, were unfamiliar to my mother's kin. My great grandmother *doña* Amelia Luna Sánchez de González (1906–1980) for example, discovered ketchup at my home at the ripe age of 75, when, one day, my mom fixed us a quick dinner of fried eggs and French fries, and *doña* Amelia asked what was the red sauce we were eating on the potatoes. "Es catsup, una salsa de tomate americana." She dipped a fry, tasted it, and liked it. "Está Buena," giving it her approval. "I will tell my daughter Cristina to buy some for her kids." She had lived some five decades on the U.S. border and had never encountered ketchup, until that night in 1976 or 1977. For some, like my great grandmother, the border is hard, fixed, impenetrable. But for others, like me and my parents, it was porous and, frankly, irrelevant.

Our familiarity with American food made us suspect to other Mexicans and brought little bits of the U.S.A. into our home. It would not be until I was older that I realized that Central Mexicans—perhaps extrapolating from their encounter with *repatriado* Mexican immigrants returned in the 1930s-1940s or braceros from the 1940s-1960s—labeled all *fronterizos* as turncoat *agringados* (*gringo*-like) or *pochos*—the word literally means *rotten* or *corrupted*, made impure by contact with foreigners—who spoke ungrammatical, English-inflected Spanish. In a colonial society, like Mexico, we police the language more, and are aware of the identities and transgressions that some dialect varieties imply. I think my parents and their families used standard Spanish and recognized regional variants, but insisted that the younger relatives maintain the language. I would not say *guayper* (wiper) or *cachus* (cashews), I had to say *limpiaparabrisas* or *nuez de la India*. We were more intentional with words. Similarly, we were intentional with the food we ate. We knew American food well. The fries were better at McD's, but the onion rings at Jack in the Box were the best. At home, when it came to Mexican food, we relished the cuisines from the interior. It was like we consumed authenticity. Housewives attempted to steal from each other servants who knew how to prepare the dishes of Jalisco, Puebla, or Veracruz (they had not yet discovered Oaxacan or Yucatecan cuisine). Good "southern cooks" (to Chihuahuans everything south of Zacatecas was "the south") were highly prized for their dexterity and ingenuity with nixtamalized corn dough, their ability to coax savory and even smoky salsas from dried peppers, and for their elaborate *moles*. Having a "southern cook" at home brought me short tasty bursts of freedom from our simple norteño fare. They brought the exotic baroque flavors to our table, a culinary reconquest, if you will, that enabled us to be safely and securely conversant in American food. At our table, the political boundary was blended, as turkey and mashed potatoes with gravy sat on the same plate as a Puebla-style picadillo that my family used for stuffing.

At age 7 or so, I would be trusted with quick errands to the market, about four blocks from our house, to fetch a pint of sour cream, some cheese, or bunch of herbs or greens, things that were needed for a new dish. The cook's desserts were also valued, but what we liked most at home were old-fashioned crystalized fruits and *jamoncillos*—a fudge-like sweet studded with piñon nuts, walnuts, or pecans. My favorite sweets have always been candied limes stuffed with chewy, juicy, sweetened coconut flakes. There were other confections, with egg liqueur (Rompope) and alcohol spiked sweet potato rolls, aptly called *borrachitos*. But dessert was not always a baroque confection. It could just as easily be quince paste (*ate de membrillo*) with a bit of cheese or shaved ice with a few drops of anise liqueur. Or fresh fruit sprinkled with chile powder, salt, and lime juice: a slice of coconut, orange quarters, cucumber slices, or jicama slivers or peeled prickly pear—*tunas*—served up cool and plain. The summer's tastiest thirst quencher.

Visits to my dad's parents' home felt like trips to the U.S. because it was a large modern house, and my grandparents served up American food. Unlike most of the houses in the city's central district, where Spanish colonial revival homes prevailed, covered in *azulejo* tiles and with heavy wrought iron fences, my father's parents lived in one of the city's oldest suburbs, from the 1940s, la *colonia ex-Hipódromo*. My grandparents' home was a big 1940s Bauhaus rambling manse, with five bedrooms, a library, a game room, large formal rooms, and huge gardens. It sat on a half of a city block and the driveway accommodated 6 or 8 cars easily. The house had originally been built by a relative of my grandmother's—Teófilo Borunda—who had been governor of Chihuahua. The walls were thick, and the windows were narrow and high up on the wall, they made the house cooler, but also safe from anyone who might want to shoot my grandfather, *don* Carlos Macías Jordán (1906–1985), who headed the police department's narcotics division. There was a rose garden in the front of the house, and in the backyard, where there had once been a small lily pond where my cousin Margarita had nearly drowned. This had been filled in with cement and fruit trees had been planted around it: pomegranates, figs, oranges, and pecans. The house smelled slightly of mothballs and orange blossom water. There were neat things all over the place—old shortwave radios, Chinese vases, books, old photos, and portraits.

At my father's parents' house we would hear dad's siblings speaking English, and my grandfather would often be in his library with friends or watching television. My grandmother, *doña* Margarita García Vásquez (1917–2020), aka *la abuela Maggie* always served iced sweet tea with lemon in the summer, and in the winter, instant coffee or hot tea. She never offered us a soft drink nor chocolate. Her cooking was eclectic and showed not only my grandfather's upbringing in the U.S., but also the influences they had encountered in church. *Don* Carlos and *doña* Maggie were Mexican Baptists. Grandfather had found it politically expedient to not be Catholic in the 1930s and 1940s—when the State and the Church feuded—when he had worked for the local government, and later, in the 1950s and 1960s, when he worked for the state government. My grandparents entertained frequently. I remember giant platters of the daintiest beef tongue spread sandwiches (a tastier version of deviled ham) wrapped in paper napkins for parties. She made desserts that I had only seen at Luby's Restaurant in El Paso—green jello mold with cottage cheese, pineapple, and pecans, or an ambrosia salad made with fruit cocktail, pistachio pudding, and marshmallows. She also made savory dishes that my dad craved but that my mother did not prepare at home, like meat loaf, roast beef, and fluffy, creamy mashed potatoes flavored with garlic and white pepper. She also made a delicious chicken in vermouth with apples, and very tasty beef *empanadas*—ground beef, bacon, olives, apples, celery, onions, raisins, pecans, and hard-boiled eggs. I really liked her fried chicken, which she coated in a mix of flour, crumbs, and spices that she dumped into a paper sack. My palate craved the food of Dixie and American Sunday dinners.

Doña Maggie did not share her recipes (or she would forget to share a couple of key steps). In the 1990s, when I was in graduate school—she must have been in her late 70s then; she died recently aged 104—she shared some of her recipes with me, including the family recipe for Christmas *bizcochitos* (a lard shortbread cookie flavored with anise seeds and sherry) and her recipes for *paella a la valenciana* and for *bacalao a la vizcaina*, which I sometimes prepare with salmon. I do not know where she learned to cook so well, but she did. It was an eclectic mix of American cooking, Spanish cuisine, and simple *norteño* Mexican fare, like pork chops with purslane, cauliflower fritters or steamed zucchini stuffed with ground beef, battered in egg white, and deep fried (*calabacitas lampreadas rellenas*). She had grown up in a large household—she had 12 siblings, two boys and eleven girls in total—and her mother, *doña* Adelaida Vásquez Stephenson (1891–1969) was reputed to have been a great cook (yes, you read that right ... my father descends from an Anglo-American fur trapper who arrived in 1818), . One of my cousins shared with me that *doña* Maggie often used recipes from a Sinaloan cookbook writer, María del Refugio "Cuca"

Fonseca de Cárdenas—but that she also learned to make a lot of dishes from her friends and acquaintances at church, and that she picked up some recipes during her travels to Europe. My mother reminded me once that *doña* Maggie was also very friendly with *doña* Rebeca Treviño de De Haro, who had owned two popular restaurants in Ciudad Juárez and Camargo, Chihuahua. Her son is high in the Chihuahuan archdiocese today. Doña Rebeca had been my parents' *madrina de lazo*—she carried the large cut crystal and mother-of-pearl rosary that was used to bind my parents together during their wedding ceremony.

On Thursdays, when the maid left early and my mother disappeared to the beauty salon to get her nails and hair done, dad would cook lunch for us. Usually, it was chili dogs or steamed buttered rice with shrimp—his favorite dishes—or he would take us out for Chinese food—pupu platter, egg rolls, and shrimp or beef chop suey. This was often followed by a movie, and a trip to the Libromex bookstore. I regularly received an allowance on Sundays from my grandfathers, and my parents also gave me money to purchase savings bonds at school, where there was a savings incentive program that we were all encouraged to participate in; you bought Banamex (National Bank of Mexico) savings stamps from the teacher and stuck them in a passbook. I did not always buy my savings stamps, so I could have money to buy books or music cassettes when we went to Libromex. I liked it because unlike other bookstores, where the books were kept behind the counter, at Libromex you could freely browse. They had a section of children's books—mostly imported from Argentina or Colombia, but not from Spain until after 1977 when trade relations were reestablished— that included beautifully illustrated histories of the ancient world. These texts were fascinating because they labeled architectural elements or parts of a sword or armor, that allowed me to build up my vocabulary. I would always double-check the oddest words in my illustrated *Pequeño Larousse* dictionary, because I had worked out that Spanish from different regions of the world was slightly different. Libromex carried subsidized popular histories and reference manuals that I enjoyed leafing through. I discovered a 20-volume cartoon history of Mexico—a joint publication of the Ministry of Education and Nueva Imagen publishers, with illustrations by Sealtiel Alatriste and the storyline by Paco Ignacio Taibo II. Each volume had a brief introduction and a section "for further reading" which I allowed me to then ask the store clerk whether they had some of those books. Often, they would have them among the two shelves dedicated to the large collection of Porrúa publishers' *Sepan Cuántos* series— which included literature and history texts—in cheap paperback editions. We thus built up a small collection of *crónicas*—first person narratives from the time of the conquest—which my father and I devoured. He taught me the pleasure of sitting to read in a comfortable chair with a good drink on the side, while listening to classical music, and would encourage me to play chess as well. I also enjoyed the musical section of Libromex, where they also sold recordings of poetry and children's fairy tales, often recorded by Spaniards, whose accents I associated with childish dreams and fantasies like the tale of the Puss in Boots—*el gato con botas*—and Thom Thumb, *Pulgarcito*.

After we left the bookstore, we would swing over three streets to pick up my freshly coiffed mother. If we walked, sometimes we would pass by the old Plaza Cervantina, which had a small stage where amateur theatre groups performed and small zarzuela recitals were held. I think these summer evening concerts were sponsored by the Ateneo Fronterizo, a cultural institution that supported the arts in the community. When we got to the salon, Mom would be by the door, her "do" covered in a headscarf to protect it for the party she would attend the next day. Sometimes she would color her hair. Her stylist was named Leonor, and she would also do her nails. After we picked her up, we would go out for a late-night dinner of *tortas*. There were three great *torta* shops we frequented then, but my favorite was Nico's which had crispy rolls, a thin schmear of refried beans, and then was loaded up with carved turkey breast or pork shoulder, topped with sliced avocado, lettuce, tomato, and delicious pickled jalapeños. Only in Mexico City have I had similar tortas; the tortas of Mexican immigrant joints in Minnesota are made with a soggy, sweet buns, low-quality meats, and lack vegetables.

We had a comfortable life in Ciudad Juárez and lived in a quaint older home whose walls were covered in *azulejo* tiles featuring scenes from around lakes Pátzcuaro and Chapala. There was a large double tiered planter and a bench also covered in *azulejos*. The home had been built in the 1920s by a distant relative of my father, one of the Flores, who had been a physician. What had been his *consultorio* was now the nursery and my parents' bedroom. That was connected to the rest of the house through the kitchen, and then there followed the living room/dining room, and two other bedrooms and bathrooms. The rooms had high ceilings and pink art deco light fixtures with brass fittings. There was a large two-car garage where my dad kept old cars—he had a 1930s Ford in there for some time. At one point in 1977 or 1978, before the bottom fell out of the Mexican economy, my parents planned to purchase a vacation home in southern New Mexico, in the cool wooded mountains above Alamogordo, in Cloudcroft. It was not going to be anything ostentatious, just a three or four bedroom weekend house where we could escape the 100-degree heat in the summer. We were three siblings then—myself, and my sisters Gloria Patricia and Fátima Lucía. The youngest, Amelia, would not be born until 1979, after we had moved to the U.S. My father owned a bus company and a bar ("La Metralla") and my mother was a housewife. Both had attended college, although my father never finished his electrical engineering degree. He was the youngest of his siblings and had learned English from them; they had crossed the border every day to attend the Lydia Patterson Institute, a United Methodist school that specialized in teaching English as a second language to the children of Mexican businessmen. My mother had spent a few years at a Catholic school for girls—El Colegio Teresiano—but at the insistence of her paternal grandmother, *doña* Amelia, her parents had enrolled her in a public school. She felt that it was a waste of money to send my mother and her sister to school there, and she did not approve of the religious education nor of the foreign language classes. "Of what use is French to them?" "The only thing," she cautioned, "that will happen is that they will become haughty like the rich girls that attend that school. They will be useless if they continue there," she declared. After mom graduated from junior high school, she trained at the Chihuahua Normal School to become a schoolteacher like her aunts and cousins. In the summers she would travel by train to Mexico City with *doña* Amelia, who accompanied her as her chaperone to sit for her exams at a National Teachers' College there. They lodged at a guest house, and after mom finished her classes, they would go out to eat and to a theatre matinee—usually a comedy or a political farce, which my grandmother enjoyed, and then out for a stroll. I get my love of Mexico City from my mother.

My father, on the other hand, hated Mexico City. Too big, too powerful, too corrupt, and just too many people. He also loathes their accents. He came from an old landowning family with deep roots in northern Mexico. On his father's side, the family hailed from Tampico; they were artists and merchants. On his mother's side the García (de Noriega) branch of the family had fled the Pueblo Revolt in New Mexico in 1680 and had settled in the Real de San Lorenzo. The other branch, the Azcárates, were relative newcomers, having arrived as soldiers and minor functionaries in the eighteenth century. Both branches received land grants, held minor administrative posts, invested in mines, and had intermarried with the first Anglo trappers who arrived in the region. They were prouder of their Basque clan—Azcárate—than of their Asturian lineage—García de Noriega—and, surprisingly, acknowledged their half-Apache great-great-grandmother, a woman from Janos. But they were otherwise colorist and disdainful of my mother's darker-skinned kin whom they described as swarthy (*prietos*). My mother's family had more money and were more educated than my father's family, but the Macías-García clan considered itself more socially prominent, had traveled to Europe and the Far East, were sophisticated, and had cousins and uncles who were high in regional and national military, political, and economic order. They owned a large dairy, a gas company, rented warehouses and factories to American and Japanese corporations, and ran other businesses. I grew up hearing my father's relatives uttering phrases like "our uncle the General," "our cousin the beauty queen," and the like. When someone was in trouble, they remembered their relatives, no matter how distant or obscure the link.

My father's family had more than its fair share of eccentrics. When they were mentioned in conversations, they added color. One cousin was a flamenco dancer, another was a painter, a great uncle had designed a biplane for the Mexican Air Force, and two cousins were so simple they were dubbed *las tontas Miranda*. My paternal grandfather's mother, Felipa Jordán Sánchez (1886–1965), had been a chorus girl (although in some tellings of the tale, she became an opera singer) and her husband Alfredo Eulogio Macías Carrillo (1880-c. 1950) had been an actor; he had been in the famed Virginia Fábregas Theatre troupe and had transitioned into early films. They traveled all over the world in the age of steamships. Their son—my grandfather *don* Carlos— was born while they were on tour, recently arrived from Cuba, in Tampico, Tamaulipas. That side of the family loved animals, and had a propensity for the exotic. My grandmother *doña* Maggie was quite an equestrian. When she was a teen, she had broken horses for her father. Don Carlos had first met her as she raced past him on a stallion. Grandma Maggie's great-great grandmother, *doña* Juana de Azcárate y Romero de Stephenson (1809–1856), came to a tragic end due to one of her animals. A pet deer, whom she had kept since it was a fawn, went into rut, charged her, gored her, and she agonized for half a night. Most of my aunts had small lap dogs with English names ("Blackie," "Fluffy"), but my dachshund was named Bellota (acorn). As an adult, I cannot understand why Americans anthropomorphize their pets and give them Spanish names. As a kid, my father—who was the youngest of his siblings—probably had the most exotic pets I had ever heard of. His father, *don* Carlos, traveled frequently and brought him a series of gifts for his menagerie: a chimp, a spider monkey, and a parakeet, all of whom, sadly, came to bitter ends. The chimp died of a cold. The female spider monkey scampered up a tree and into the electric cables where it died; her name was *Chita* (Cheeta). The parakeet flew into a washing machine whence it emerged plucked, pink, and stiff. From that point on, father was only given dogs. As he got older and wealthier, he acquired pedigreed canines—so expensive that my mother feuded with him over their cost and upkeep. I remember two English Pointers that we took on our hunting trips to the Chihuahuan sierra. Lovely dogs—but they ate their weight in food and never did manage to retrieve the game birds we shot.

My mother's paternal side was typical of those lower-middle class families who had risen in the world thanks to the Mexican Revolution. They profited from access to opportunity, public education, the expansion of the state bureaucracy, and government subsidies to boost the urban food supply, but although they lived on the U.S. border, they had little interest on what was on the other side of the boundary. My great grandparents struggled—doña Amelia lost half of her babies to illness, but six survived childhood. My great grandfather Manuel González Carrillo (1899–1950) died from diabetes complications, just a few years after relocating to Ciudad Juárez from Torreón, Coahuila, where he had been a baker. They hailed originally from Zacatecas; she was from Fresnillo and he was from Jeréz. Men in his family, the González clan, had been bakers for centuries. My mother's paternal aunts and uncles included a pharmacist, a nurse, teachers, a college counselor, and an accountant. Only one studied in the U.S. and learned English—aunt Socorro, who became a nurse. The rest remained Mexican and Spanish monolingual. They had humble beginnings, one of many migrant families that flocked to the border in the 1930s and lived in rented lodgings. My great grandfather had initially done well for himself in Juárez and educated his eldest well, paying for schooling in the U.S. But in time, he became ill, the diabetes treatment ate up their savings, and he died. My grandfather, *don* Manuel, was the second oldest, and he helped his widowed mother and siblings. They rented a bakery from a Spanish immigrant woman and eventually bought the property. Grandfather's older brother, Jesús, abandoned them to their luck. He had become a pharmacist, married well, and was embarrassed of them, as they sold bread on the street and in the buses. Almost a decade passed before the family reconciled. By the mid-1950s, my grandfather bought a new car every year and took his family on vacations to central Mexico or to the U.S. My mother and her siblings visited Disneyland in the late 1950s and early 1960s. In Anaheim, they visited relatives who had left Ciudad Juarez in the 1940s and settled there. Grandfather moved his mother and younger siblings to a nice home with a garden and provided for their schooling and marriages. Grandfather bought out the Spanish woman, knocked down the old bakery and raised a new building, two-storied, with a basement. On the ground floor, he had two retail spaces, a workshop, and bathrooms. He rented out one of the retail spaces—that was his mother's pin money. Upstairs, he built apartments. The basement was a warehouse for flour, oil, shortening, and sugar. A cat prowled the premises. Don Manuel's siblings all lived in large suburban homes in beautiful neighborhoods with two-car garages, green manicured lawns, live-in maids, and living rooms with fake fireplaces and Last Supper prints in gilt frames. Family parties featured live music—mariachis or string trios—and mounds of grilled beef or a copper kettle full of *carnitas* and *chicharrones*, with giant *piñatas*, huge themed cakes, customized party favor bags full of American candy bars, and clown emcees that led the kids in games but also told ribald jokes for the adults' amusements.

Uncle Francisco Fernando, who was an accountant and worked for the *Secretaría de Hacienda* (the Mexican IRS), also owned a bakery. He loved gadgets and was a good photographer. He made home movies and it is a pity they have all been lost. My grandfather's oldest sister, Aunt Socorro, was a nurse; the other sisters were Consuelo, Cristina, and Concepción. Consuelo had studied to be an executive secretary, but when she showed up for a job interview at the Centro Escolar Revolución, she found the position had been filled. The staff liked her and felt sorry for her, so they offered her a job as a first-grade teacher; they told her she had a commanding presence and dressed well, and that they would give her the lesson plans. She stayed. Over the years, she taught all of her nieces and nephews to read and write—including me. She married a baker, Jesús Díaz. Her sister Cristina became a high school teacher and married a colleague from Veracruz, Arturo Navarrete. The youngest, Conchita, had wanted to become a nurse, but her mother did not like that she had to spend nights at the hospital, so she became a biologist. She taught high school briefly, but then became a college counselor. She married a professor, Héctor Olave; they became my godparents. He later became dean and served on the city council. He was an engineer.

My mother's maternal family, the Nápoles Barrón clan, has a fascinating history crossing class, racial, and national borders. Mother's maternal grandfather, *don* Antonio Nápoles Cortés (1890–1980), was blond and blue-eyed. He was as pale as his wife, my great grandmother Librada Barrón Zambrano (1902–1973) was dark. She was probably Afro-mestiza, given her rural origins in Zacatecas, a mining district that had been the backbone of Mexico in the colonial period, when enslaved Blacks had been taken there to alleviate the labor shortage during the silver bonanza. The family's vocabulary to describe the resulting hues of *don* Antonio and *doña* Librada's offspring was comparable to that of a viceregal *pintura de casta*, colorism was alive and well. They hailed from the Hacienda de Tlacotes, close to Ojocaliente. Her parents and siblings fled from there to the border during the Revolution. She and her parents were illiterate, although her brothers and a sister knew how to write their names. Doña Librada only signed with an X, and her younger brother Saturnino was blind.

Don Antonio hailed from provincial Spanish families in Morelia, Michoacán, who had moved to Mexico City after the Wars of the Reform in the 1850s. His grandfather had been a candlemaker, and his father, Onésimo Nápoles Lomelín (1843–1916) was a mechanic who became a pioneer electrical engineer. For a time the Nápoles lived in central Mexico City, in rented rooms. His children were born all over Mexico as he and his young wife, Concepción Cortés Ojeda (1861–1896) moved around the country installing the first power plants, beginning with the Mexico City power plant in 1897 and the Necaxa plant of the Mexican Light and Power Company in 1903. My great-grandfather was one of a dozen children of his father's first marriage, and when his mother died of Tuberculosis in 1896, he did not reconcile himself to his step-mother, so he ran away from home. Antonio made his way north, arrived in Ciudad Juárez in the final years of the Porfiriato. He had completed elementary school and had beautiful handwriting. He worked as a mechanic, then a chauffeur, and clerked for the railroad, before working at the Federal Customs House in Juárez. I remember visiting him at his cubicle in the building's main hall in the mid-1970s, shortly before he retired—and the building was closed down and transformed into a museum. Don Antonio was autodidact. He read on a variety of topics, but enjoyed history and collected stamps, coins, and had many newspaper clippings. He spoke softly, had an elegant air about him, and I adored visiting him to chat about history, especially the Revolution. He traveled in the summers to visit his siblings in Mexico City, Puebla, and Chiapas. A younger brother, Edmundo, was an engineer, who had married a niece of President Cárdenas. They lived in Mexico City.

Don Antonio and his wife *doña* Librada met in the 1920s, during the government's feud with the Church, so they never celebrated their matrimony; they only had a civil ceremony, something that pained doña Librada's mother, my great-great grandmother Rita Zambrano Elías (1866–1939), who was a devout Catholic. They had many children, of whom only seven survived. Most of the men worked as bartenders or taxi drivers, profiting from the city's tourism. My great grandmother died of diabetes in 1973. What I know of her, I heard from her youngest sister, my great aunt Felícitas (1910–2000), who had worked as a housekeeper to a Lebanese family in El Paso. After she retired, she helped out my mother with me and my sister. She told us many stories about *doña* Librada and her family. She made us laugh mocking her sister's country speech—she never learned to speak proper urban Spanish; she used to say *hiprioquita* in lieu of *hipócrita*, for example. She could not read but enjoyed looking at the cartoons in the newspapers before she cut them into small pieces for use in the bathroom. When my grandfather worked for the railroad and the customs service, grandmother used to amass large quantities of foodstuffs that my grandfather brought home from work—bribes, I imagine—and she would save them and take them with her to her cousins, who had remained at the old hacienda of Tlacotes, to feed them. The communal farms the Revolution had carved out of the lands of the old hacienda never produced much, and people barely survived. The sacks of beans, rice, sugar, and flour that doña Librada brought and distributed from the border were a lifeline for some two dozen kin folk who celebrated her arrival as Christmas. She knew what their needs were from messages she received, by word of mouth from the poor starving family friends who showed up every so often, knowing that *doña* Librada and *don* Antonio had a bowl of beans and some tortillas for travel-weary migrants who came to the border looking for work. She had tortillas and beans on the stove all day long to feed her many children, neighbors, and friends. No one left her neat rambling adobe house hungry. They reminded her of her own trek north during the Revolution and of her older sister Trinidad's immigrant experience in the mining camps of Colorado in the 1910s and 1920s. Once you had a foot-hold on the border, she thought, she had to help others passing north or south. Her generosity lives on in the work we all do to aid the less fortunate.

My parents' privilege meant that they could access U.S.-health care at a time when the largest hospitals in Ciudad Juárez were either the Municipal General Hospital—for the indigent—or the Federally-funded Social Security clinics where bureaucrats and workers received their care. Small private clinics in Juárez were expensive and demanded payment in cash up front, so people like my parents birthed their children on the installment plan at private clinics across the river in El Paso. My mother chose Newark Methodist Hospital where her aunt Socorro worked as a nurse. My sisters were later born at the more posh Providence Memorial Hospital—originally established by El Paso's Jewish community. My mother took us there for our vaccines and regular check-ups. However, the physician into whose care she entrusted us when we became sick was Dr. Antonio Villalva Sosa, who lived some 15 blocks from our house. He had trained in the U.S. after finishing medical school in Mexico City. His waiting room was large and there were regularly 15 or 20 mothers with crying babies waiting to see him. My parents liked him a lot, especially since he never gouged them. Once, another physician diagnosed a lower abdominal pain that I had as appendicitis. Mother took me to see Dr. Villalva, who dismissed his colleague's diagnosis and treated me for a urinary tract infection instead. He treated my sisters' earaches, sore throats, and colds.

Another way that the border was permeable was television. American tele-vision programs—CBS, ABC, NBC, and PBS—came into our home. This was before cable. We watched television in English before we learned the language. In addition to the Saturday morning cartoons, my sisters and I watched three programs with regularity: "The Wonderful World of Disney" and Mutual of Omaha's "Wild Kingdom" on NBC, and the "Lawrence Welk Show" on PBS. We did not need much English to appreciate those programs, or the old Western movies that regularly came on in the afternoons. I did need my father's help to watch historic television series, such as "Centennial" (1978) an NBC mini-series that featured the history of Colorado. We watched it in bed with our parents—it was on Sunday nights over the Fall and Spring of 1978–1979. Dad would interpret between scenes. He had studied English in junior high school in Juárez, but had also grown up hearing it spoken by his siblings who had studied in El Paso at the Lydia Patterson Institute. Father, who had only studied in Mexican schools, has a strong accent when he speaks English, unlike his siblings who studied in the U.S. He learned it from books, and from teachers who did not speak it very well. He attempts to pronounce every letter, as in Spanish. Salmon, one of our favorite fish, always has an *L* when my father pronounces the word, and he cannot tell the difference between a *ch* and a *sh* sound. Now that he spends a lot of time with my nephews, who are primarily English speakers, his English has improved. But I did not know that when I was a kid and we were still living in Mexico. Every other Sunday, we would visit father's aunt Natalia in El Paso. She fixed great dinners—I was very fond of her baked enchiladas, but I also loved it when she served fried chicken— and after dinner, we would watch a movie on television, eating oranges or ice cream as we did. ABC ran its "Movie of the Week" then; I think we viewed most of the James Bond 007 films in this way, with dad or Natalia's husband, uncle Manuel Ramos, interpreting. The American television programs enriched the viewing options on the two Mexican channels we watched at home most of the time. They made me curious about the world beyond, and they fed my curiosity about U.S. history, which I did not know much about. The scanty clothing and lax moral ways of Americans on television programs confirmed the stereotypes that relatives held about *gringos*: the women were sexually promiscuous, the men were drunks, their diet consisted of cold sandwiches and burgers, and they did not care for the family, as their children moved out without finishing school or getting married, and, thus, they placed their elderly into old folks' homes. My mother and her friends would often impart advice to their younger male relatives: "don't marry a white girl, they don't care well for their men, that's why they divorce and take drugs."

Television and radio enriched what I knew about languages, Mexican culture, and the world beyond, allowing me to transcend many borders, not just that between El Paso and Juárez. We had many television and radio sets at home. The largest television set was in the parlor, some 26-inches across or so. It was in its own self-contained piece of furniture, with long legs. It was massive—and it took a while to come on and for the image to focus. I watched it sitting on the red leather sofas or stretched out on a towel on the parquet floor with a cushion. If I wanted to change the channel, I had to get up and switch the knob manually—but I had to make sure I had washed my hands if I did so. Mom kept a Kleenex box on top to remind me, next to the rabbit-ear antenna that sat atop the set, with a large dial to adjust the image. My parents had a remote-control color television in their bedroom; it had doors that could be closed to protect the screen and that helped it to stand out less amid the heavy pecan bedroom furniture. The remote control itself was large, about the size of a small box of animal crackers. It was black plastic and chrome. I was not allowed to touch it. There was a smaller black-and-white television set in the guest bedroom, where I would sneak in to watch it when mom was watching something else in the parlor. It was yellow plastic and had metallic knobs; when it overheated, the image flickered. In the kitchen, on the counter next to the stove, my parents kept a smaller black-and-white television set; it was a portable television that we would take camping. We watched the Mexico City morning news on it while having breakfast, although after 9 AM, my parents generally had the radio on in the kitchen. I think they thought it caused less of a distraction. I do recall hearing reruns of *radionovelas* (radio soap operas) like "Porfirio Cadena, el ojo de vidrio" a melodrama set in rural northern Mexico and comedy skits like "La Tremenda Corte," which featured the antics of a Cuban *pícaro* who ran afoul of the law and ended up in court to defend his actions. These were broadcast on radio XEJ 960 or XEFV 1000 "La Rancherita," or XEWG 1240. We also listened to the radio at night; there was an investigative journalist who engaged in political polemics that my parents followed. We were, after all, living in a one-party regime where torture and disappearances occurred, not that I knew much about that as a child, beyond the occasional references in adults' conversations or the handbills I found strewn on the sidewalk when I went to the market or bakery. These were distributed by committees of parents of the disappeared and bore the name of Rosario Ibarra de Piedra, who organized the *Comité Eureka* in 1977 to agitate on behalf of political prisoners. I thought about this as something that happened elsewhere, as I did not know much about the reasons behind the appearance of a new paramilitary force— the *Boinas Negras* (black caps)—who appeared in groups of two or three and struck fear into people.

Despite the appeal of American television, its influence on me was relatively limited to Saturday mornings and Sunday afternoons and evenings. Mexican television and radio had a heavier impact on me, as it blared at home most of the week. We had four televisions, two radios (one had short wave radio), and a large stereo at home. The maids told me I was lucky because they did not have television at home; they had to pay a neighbor to let them watch their soap operas at night. Our televisions and radios kept us connected to news and culture in central Mexico, but also opened a window to the world, to developments across Latin America, and to Europe. From a young age, listening to news and programs, I knew that there were different Spanish-language dialects and accents. I could tell there were even different regional accents within Mexico and in Spain. I also had heard the languages of Mexico's indigenous peoples. A local radio station broadcast messages early in the morning in Rarámuri—the

language of the Tarahumaras, relaying messages of travelers' safe arrivals at
the border or the need for medicine. I could even tell the difference in the
accents of different Spaniards—cultured urban intellectuals from Madrid did
not sound like the poor Galician bakers or successful Asturian shopkeepers
who appeared as stock characters on radio and television programs, but that I
also knew in real life. What I did not learn until I was over 9 or 10 was that there
were significant differences in American English; I knew that Britons spoke
differently from Americans (I saw a certain parallel between Mexico's relationship to Spain and the U.S.'s relationship to its mother country). Authorities
in central Mexico communicated with us *fronterizos* well through the media;
on Sundays, the Televisa television monopoly carried a cheesy variety show
"Siempre en Domingo" ("Always on Sunday," which many of us ridiculed by
calling it "Always the Same Shit," "Siempre lo mismo") which featured the latest
boy bands and crooners, but also travel segments that showed the rich diversity of Mexico's regions, and featured local dances and folk singers. After that
program ended, all the radios across Mexico broadcast "La Hora Nacional," a
program that had been designed in the 1930s to engage in national building
and ideological indoctrination. It combated anti-government attitudes and
broadcast the ideals of national culture. The format included folk music, skits,
informational capsules on historical topics, and updates on national health,
hygiene, and educational campaigns. The same program was on every radio
station across the country at 10 PM on Sundays. You could not escape it. My
parents and their friends did not care much for the program; they saw right
through it, but they liked to hear the folk music and stories.

Channel 2 from Mexico City, carried the Televisa signal, and channel 5, XEJ,
was a locally-owned television station that produced much of its programming
and ran dubbed programs. Channel 5 was the third-oldest television station
outside of Mexico City and first went on the air in 1954. It was owned by a
radio and television pioneer, don Pedro Meneses Hoyos. Their weekly variety
programs featured local talent and helped launch many careers; I did not care
much for it because it was mostly ranchero music. I preferred their afternoon
program, hosted by clown Niko Liko, who had talent contests, cake and movie
pass giveaways, and showed old "Mighty Mouse" cartoons. I think they also
had old eastern bloc children's programming as well, like "Bolek and Lolek."
The studios were not far from our home in an old theatre on the Benito Juárez
Monument square, and my sister Gloria and our neighbor Claudia once put
together a dance routine and lip-synched to some disco number, wearing
matched outfits. The talent shows were popular and I am sure most girls aged
five to twelve enjoyed them. Some of these performances included boys as
well, but I was not interested. Channel 5 also carried old Spanish and Mexican

movies for children, including one about Robinson Crusoe, the "Pili y Mili" adventure movies, and a series of films featuring actors clad in horrid fur costumes of foxes, cats, and squirrels who ranged about the forests of Spain doing good, saving damsels, and assisting the *Guardia Civil* rural constabulary.

Channel 2 carried news programs in the morning, followed by game shows—which fascinated me, especially all the brands of toys or electronic equipment that were advertised but which were not sold in Ciudad Juárez. These were a reminder of how the border region was chronically under-supplied and we had to make most of our furniture and household electronics in El Paso, and then smuggle the items back into Mexico, making a sport of avoiding import duties. After the morning news, Channel 2 carried variety programs, and we sometimes watched Chef Chepina Peralta, Mexico's answer to Julia Child, whose 15-minute segments provided housewives with economic and nutritious recipes. Truth be told, my mother rolled her eyes at Chef Chepina's use of ingredients or techniques that were not available along the border. She disliked crepes—which she had never made since my father preferred pancakes—and had never cared for Huitlacoche (corn fungus). But what I really liked was the afternoon programming. Channel 2 carried Mexican and Spanish films, black and white classics from the 1940s to the 1960s, with occasional color films. The films introduced me to Mexico's legendary artists—Sara García, the Soler brothers, Jorge Negrete, Pedro Infante, Luis Aguilar, Dolores del Río, Lilia Prado, Elsa Aguirre, Joaquín Pardavé, María Félix, Arturo de Córdova, Angélica María, César Costa—but also to the idealized Mexico of the 1890s-1950s that those movies portrayed, reinforcing my nascent aesthetic sense. There were also Argentine and Spanish actresses, many of whom sang my favorite songs: Libertad Lamarque, Mary Santpere, and Sara Montiel. I found Spanish films appealing. I liked opera and zarzuela, and I really enjoyed Montiel's "El último cuplé" (1957) and "La Violetera" (1958), with their sumptuous costumes, and idealization of Spain and things Spanish. It reinforced stereotypes of Spanish culture acquired from going to the bullfights with my grandfather or eating paella on Sundays at La Sevillana—a Spanish restaurant run by a family of exiled republicans, the Tabuencas, whom I would later befriend in college—and clouded my perception of Franco's dictatorship. But the films also nursed an anticipation and curiosity about Spain in a way that was different from what I felt towards the U.S. Because I was already familiar with the U.S., I consumed the history of the U.S., but not knowing much about Spain—and especially about its precipitous drop in global stature—I became more curious about Spain. I hazily remember the death of General Franco being reported by Jacobo Zabludovsky—a Jewish Mexican news anchor who wore his trademark large frame glasses and big headphones. For weeks on end, Zabludovsky commented on Franco's health, and the same image was broadcast of him wearing an oxygen mask. I remember being told to stand at attention when his death was finally acknowledged. After relations with Spain were reestablished—they had been handled by the Cubans previously—we began to see more Spanish goods, books, and movies, but on Televisa there were also correspondents who reported on events in Spain during the transition after Franco. I remember coverage of don Juan Carlos I and doña Sofía's state visit to Mexico in 1977 and the emotional coverage of the return of many republican exiles to Spain. By then, in the second grade, I followed these developments in the newspapers as well.

But I am getting ahead of myself. I was a precocious learner, thanks to my mother, who taught me to read and write before I went to kindergarten. I had a notebook and pencils, and I liked to sit at a table or desk to draw and write. I liked to write poetry, or so I thought, composing rhyming couplets that I gifted my sister or cousins on birthdays. Kindergarten was wonderful. There were no boys to play with at home—when I was small, my mother would not let me out of our house on to the street out of fear of the speeding cars passing by. I was restricted to play by myself, so I made elaborate costumes and headgear from paper grocery sacks. I was a pharaoh, or a bishop, an emperor, a prince. But I always reigned over a kingdom of a rebellious, chaotic inhabitant, my baby sister, who did not obey my commands. Hence, Kindergarten let me socialize with other children. The school, Jardín de Niños Federal Benito Juárez, had originally been a convent school attached to our parish, El Sagrado Corazón de Jesús. The state had seized it in the 1930s and turned it into a showcase school. We had lots of supplies and equipment, and our teachers organized outings to markets and workshops so we could see sculptors and artists at work. In the garden there was a covered sandbox, where I and a few of the more quiet, softer boys played while the rowdies ran and scampered about. I grew attached to a pale green-eyed blond kid—I think his name was Claudio—who ran towards me the moment I arrived and we played and sat together all the time. I shared my snacks with him. We were inseparable friends. His parents noticed how close we were and I talked about nothing but him when I got home. Claudio this and Claudio than. After he left, I was sad, but one day my teacher gave my mother an invitation from his parents. I got to see him again at his birthday party. His parents were rich! He had amusement park rides in his backyard and the home was huge, at least three or four times the size of ours. He had a clown at his party and we played, but things were not the same. He had other friends and cousins at this party. I eventually forgot about Claudio by the end of the year, when my parents announced that I would enroll at the Centro Escolar Revolución, a Federal elementary school that had been built by President Lázaro Cárdenas in the late 1930s. My teacher was to be my great aunt Consuelo. In the morning, my grandfather don Manuel would pick me up at home in his big car—a yellow Ford Crown Victoria with a white top and white wall wheels—and dropped me off at school. Through the first grade, my parents would pick me up. I would wait outside the school under the shade of a tree. Occasionally they would forget to pick me up, which produced anxiety and nervous crying fits. My aunt Consuelo, who was my teacher, did not put up with it. After one too many of these episodes, she asked me, "Did your mother die? Boys only cry when their mothers die." I cried even harder at the thought of my mother's death. Then she slapped me. Hard. Once, twice, thrice, all the while repeating "Boys don't cry."

Around the first and second grade, I began spending more time with my maternal grandfather, *don* Manuel González Luna. I love my father very much, but as he was always at work, I spent more time with *don* Manuel, who incidentally, preferred to call me by my second name, Manuel, which was the same as his own. Grandpa was very tall, I remember him towering over all other men, and he was very elegant. He wore a tie, with a cardigan, and a coat. He was diabetic and suffered from open wounds on his feet, so he limped a bit and spent most of the day at the bakery seated with his feet up. In the evening, when he got home, my grandmother Josefina cleaned his wounds and replaced his bandages. He did not wear shoes, he wore slippers everywhere, to better accommodate the heavy dressings. He had poor eyesight—another symptom of his diabetes—and this made driving difficulty for him, but he still drove. He told me to tell him if any children were on the street so he could slow down and beep. He and grandma Josefina lived in the suburbs, in a white brick American ranch style house with double French doors, with weeping willows and large flower beds. She babysat me whenever my parents were out of town or busy with a big social event. I loved being there because grandma Josefina let me play in her big back yard. She would let me irrigate all the trees, and I would build canals and dams, and fleets of paper boats to launch upon them. Grandma Josefina loved flowers—her favorite were gardenias—and she spent most of her day at home, caring for my youngest aunt and uncle. We had many of our birthday parties there since the gardens were large and there was so much street parking. When we had sleepovers, she made delicious breakfasts—my favorite were *enfrijoladas*—and we would go to the supermarket nearby.

By the time I started the second grade, my grandfather *don* Manuel insisted that I walk to his bakery after school, where I could help him out, and then he would drive me home, frequently staying to lunch. The bakery was only 4 blocks away, along a heavily transited route where there were shops, barbers, a carpenter, one bar, and two newspaper kiosks that distracted me and lengthened my commute by at least five minutes. The daily hour or two with my grandfather became quite the education for me. He groomed me for life, taught me to deal with customers, to respect workers, and to manage money. His own sons, my uncles, had by then decided not to work with him as he had a short temper and was a strict disciplinarian. They helped in the evening instead, when grandfather had already gone home—and the volume of sales increased. As he drove me to school, *don* Manuel talked to me about the day's work. When I got to the bakery after school, he put me to clean the trays and rearrange the morning bread and to take out the afternoon bake. I also rang up customers. I would show him the customer's tray of bread and pastries, he would add up the total in his head, and I would bag the purchase, then ring up cash. I did a lot of math in my head—my mother drilled me at my multiplication tables—so I noticed that grandfather charged different prices. I asked him to explain to me why he did that. He told me to close the bakery doors first, and explained how he read customers, to listen to their speech, to look at their clothing and how they clutched their money before deciding whether to over- or under-charge them. A mother with three kids in tow and patches on their pants that only bought bread rolls and a single sweet roll would pay less than a young male factory worker who was out to impress his girlfriend and purchased only expensive cakes. I remember him giving free milk to the poor mother of three. He told me to look at dress, make up, and jewelry, but also behavior and demeanor, especially to see how carefully people counted money. Most of the customers were also waiting outside for the bus that would take them home, so some would put bread back to have enough money to cover their fare. The operation was facilitated by the baroque price structure; the government subsidized and dictated low prices for some items but not all, and buns that had additional twists and turns (more bakers' labor) were more expensive. Occasionally there were tourists—American GI s from Fort Bliss in El Paso who were out for a good time and wandered in to buy rolls or a cake, or older married Anglo couples, day trippers who were out to "see Mexico." They stared at all the buns and rolls, and often did not buy. They irked my grandfather. "They only come in here to gawk at food! Why don't you buy, try the bread, so you know what it tastes like!" he would shout at the nervous smiling tourists who did not understand the older man's ire. The most adventurous would buy the large, iced crocodiles and turtles (raisins for eyes, cookie dough for a shell, orange blossom flavored dough underneath).

My grandfather also taught me to deal with the bank and occasionally had me accompany him to collect rent. School let out at 1. At 1.30, I raced to the Banco Longoria down the street to drop off the previous day's sales. Often, my grandfather would call ahead and let the bank manager know that I was coming late. When I got to the bank, a teller would be waiting for me and accept the deposit from me. As she counted, I would lick the small sucker she had handed me. I carried the cash in a large, zippered bag that had the bank's logo on it. I held it tightly at my chest, wrapped in a paper sack, and walked carefully the three blocks to the bank. By the end of the second grade, I was also counting the money and filled out the deposit slip. Deposits on Monday were large; they had the Saturday and Sunday sales, which included also cake orders. On Mondays I easily deposited US $1,500 or more. Grandfather had two accounts at the Banco Longoria. One was kept in Mexican pesos, the other was in U.S. dollars; many of his customers worked in the U.S. or received money from there, so they paid in greenbacks. The dollar account was used to purchase supplies in El Paso that were cheaper or of better quality than those in Mexican stores. We purchased cake boxes, baking sheets, cupcake wrappers, paper sacks, and gigantic rolls of waxed paper. After we were done at the bank and the bakery, we would drive home, stopping occasionally to collect rent— he owned about four or five rental properties with apartments and commercial spaces—and I would get down from the car and go knock on doors to collect the rent. I would pound hard on the door and ask the person to come to the car, where my grandfather waited patiently. He would give them receipts for the cash we collected. We stopped occasionally at a barber shop, where he would get shaved, have his fingernails trimmed and buffed, and get a neat trim. The shaving ritual seemed complicated, with steaming towels wrapped on his face, hot water poured from a coffee percolator into a mug where the barber worked up a lather with a brush, and then grab a strap of leather to sharpen the razor's blade, and then moved quickly and efficiently across my grandfather's face, grabbing his skin taught, stretching it, holding the razor at the right angle to produce a clean, smooth shave. He would wipe his face when done, apply lavender or orange blossom *eau de toilette*, and scented powder. I would also get a trim, sitting on a board placed over the barber's chair, and constantly tremble because the electric razor's vibrations would overstimulate me. I looked like my grandfather's *doppelgänger* once the barber was done with me. He would drop me off at home and then he would go play dominos for the rest of the evening at his club. He was president of the Bullfighting Aficionados. The group attracted other Mexican businessmen but also Mexican American businessmen and professionals as well as some Spaniards. After he finished, he would return home, and he would receive his friends. I really enjoyed listening to him talk with Professor Armando B. Chávez M., who had served in the Mexican legislature, taught history at the local university, and had been *cronista* or official historian of our city. He asked me whether I had seen the history mural at city hall, and I asked him to tell me about Indian raids. I loved his visits because he often brought copies of his latest books as gifts. Grandfather had helped him with a large donation to build a junior high school for working class kids.

Early in the summer, with the dollar bank account buoyant with profits from Mother's Day cake sales, *don* Manuel would take me clothes shopping, a great wad of cash in his coat pockets. I was the eldest grandson, born of his oldest daughter, and he doted on me like he never had on his own sons. We would spend an entire afternoon at the Farah's Suit Factory—a large series of warehouses in south El Paso that employed hundreds of seamstresses. The salesman—who was an acquaintance from his club—would know ahead of time that we were coming and would have a selection of suits for me to try on. They were three-piece polyester and wool suits, long-lasting, which sometimes came with a second pair of pants. The vests were reversible. The colors were always the same: a dark suit for funerals, a pinstriped suit for weddings or Sundays, and a light-colored suit—usually tan or light brown—to wear on other occasions. He would also purchase a linen short-sleeved leisure suit that I could wear to parties in the summer, and a couple of short-sleeved guayaberas. The long-sleeved ones that he favored had French cuffs, and he did not think that was practical for me. A half dozen colorful shirts (it was the mid-1970s) and a handful of ties—usually purchased from the bargain basement at The Popular Dry Goods Department Store in El Paso—finished off the wardrobe. My mother would purchase my shoes—and matching belts—at Thom McAn's and my underwear and pajamas at the Children's mezzanine in JCPenney's. My dad's mom, Grandma Maggie, usually gifted me two packages of Gold Toe "fluffies" on Christmas or my birthday, ever practical and frugal. I would get my winter coats from Levine's or Rosen's in downtown El Paso. They always had leather or fur trim on thick gabardine or wool coats. Barring the occasional *guayabera* and the black leather oxfords from Tres Hermanos shoe stores, I did not wear a single item of Mexican-made clothing. It was all imported from the U.S. I don't think I ever wore a pair of Mexican underwear until my mother acquired an itchy polyester thing for me at a sale when Coloso opened a department store in downtown Juárez in 1979. My husband looks at my childhood photographs and chuckles: "You were a regular Little Lord Fauntleroy. Did you have silver buckles too?"

By the time I reached the third grade, 1978, the economy had begun to deteriorate affecting how my parents spent their income. My father's businesses continued to be profitable, but since his income was in pesos, it increasingly took more and more pesos to buy the same amount or quality of goods in El Paso stores. The proportion of American goods we consumed in our household decreased as the peso was devalued and our budget could no longer stretch as far. Significant wealth flowed into Mexico from new oil discoveries, but the amount of money that had to be borrowed abroad to develop new refineries and seaports led to a negative balance of payments and the population was expanding rapidly. Corruption and inefficiencies decreased the amount and quality of food that was produced in Mexico, so more had to be imported; this created a shortage of foreign currency. The business community lost faith in a government that had populist policies and refused to make necessary budget cuts; capital flight increased. My grandfather bought up as many dollars as he could and stashed money abroad, knowing that a financial crisis would hit. By 1978 or 1979 there were stricter limits on how much Mexican shoppers could spend abroad—you could not legally import back more than US $25 in groceries per trip, and larger purchases had to pay an import duty, which in practice meant you had to bribe the customs officer to look the other way. With more Mexicans being forced to purchase more of their food in Mexico, larger, nicer grocery stores began to appear in Ciudad Juárez, where we could purchase American goods—at a significant mark up—or where we acquired Mexican canned goods and packaged food. My aunts and uncles who were public servants weathered the shortages somewhat better, since their labor unions opened shops that catered to them; they seemed better stocked and had goods sent to them from central Mexico, while the stores open to the general public made do with northern Mexican manufactured goods or U.S. imports. Perhaps this is why I over-buy groceries and I stash extra jars of marmalade, syrup, juice and oil in our basement pantry. We never went without, thank God, but I think the anxiety of shortages stayed with me.

Around 1978 or 1979, we purchased Mexican toiletries for the first time, which seemed harsher and more strongly scented. Toilet paper was not as soft nor as colorful. Mexican toothpaste seemed too sweet and was only available in mint flavor—if you could find it at all. It tended to ooze out of cracks that developed in the tube as you rolled it up. As more and more people purchased goods in Juárez, shortages became frequent, and limits were placed on how much one could buy. Mexican Americans were also showing up at the stores because they discovered they could make their dollar go further in Juárez. Things that were heavily subsidized by the government—certain cuts of meat, sugar, salt, rice, pasta, beans—frequently ran out because, as inflation set in, people hoarded these items. Even grandfather *don* Manuel was unable to get enough butter, sugar, and eggs for his bakery. I spent many afternoons queueing in various shops to purchase a half-kilo of sugar, for example, which the state-owned enterprises had restricted from circulating because they wanted to export as much as possible to earn foreign currency. By the early 1980s, items in the stores no longer had their prices; they instead had codes that the clerks used to look up on pricing lists where, as inflation grew during the day, the prices were regularly adjusted. We had always circumvented these shortages due to our relative affluence, and now, for the first time, we experienced the privations that were common among the masses. Except, because we knew that those things existed on the other side of the border—five-pound bags of sugar, unlimited cheap canned goods, jumbo bags of cereal, cheap fast food, nice clothes, soft toilet paper—the shortages seemed harder. The same border that had once given us access to this abundance now seemed impenetrable without access to dollars and given the strict restrictions placed on how much we could import back to Mexico. At the bank, businessmen could have access to dollars at a subsidized exchange rate to import spare parts or equipment, but the rest of us had to pay the higher free-floating exchange that began to inch up as capital flight mounted. In 1976, the dollar had increased from $12.50 to $22.50. By 1982, it jumped $150 to 1, and by 1988, it reached $2,300. We could still go shopping in the U.S., but we did so mainly to stare, to window shop (an aunt called it "baba-shopping," that is, "drool shopping"—because you only had $25 dollars to spend per household and you had to be judicious in what you purchased—so you drooled at the thought of what you could have but ultimately could not acquire. So the money we could spend abroad was limited to absolute necessities—baby formula, diapers, medicine, food items in short supply, and other things that could not be found in Mexico. I think we resented Americans and Mexican Americans, who suddenly seemed rich and bought up the nicer cuts of beef and the seafood at the grocery stores. Within three years, how I related to life on the border took a great turn, from one of abundance and ease, to one of shortages and anxiety. These feelings would only increase when we moved to the United States—*pero esa, es otra historia.*

PART 2

Wild Tongues

∵

CHAPTER 5

Criterion Number 3

Unstable Sense of Self; ca. 1993

Paul Pedroza

When I was twelve, I wanted to be a marine biologist. I didn't know how to swim then, and I still don't, but I'd discovered a love of wildlife—sea life, in particular—thanks to the discount glossy books I found at stores like Pic 'n' Save. I'd flip through them over and over, ignoring the text after a couple of half-hearted shots at reading the difficult biological descriptions, spellbound by ocean life, a world so different from mine, something I'd finally see for myself in the summer of 1993 when my family and I visited Savannah, Georgia. I was so devoted to that ocean life that I made it known to everyone that I'd return to the coast in a few years so that I could earn my degree and then set sail for the benefit of all fish, marine mammals, and sea flora.

The urge to explore the shadowy regions of the world's oceans became my sixth-grade obsession, and I'd spend some of my sixth-grade lunches waiting for the library to reopen for the afternoon so that I could enjoy all of the marine biology books I couldn't afford to own. I don't remember the reason why the library wasn't open the entire school day. All I remember is the exquisite alone time I'd enjoy, if I could only endure the usual gauntlet before those doors opened.

∴

Criterion number three is but one of nine possible symptoms you may exhibit if you live with borderline personality disorder, or BPD. It isn't required that you exhibit all nine, just five, and this results in 256 unique combinations. My particular number of symptoms is seven, down from eight thanks to certain dialectical behavior therapy techniques. The possibility of so many unique takes results in varying and specific profiles, which can make an accurate diagnosis difficult. It's estimated that 10% of the population lives with this particular personality disorder. Historically, BPD has been diagnosed more often for women, though it's believed that the number of men who live with it is roughly the same, because men have been misdiagnosed or ignored, they've been hesitant to seek treatment, or they've ended up in prisons and graveyards because of their undiagnosed condition. Suicidal ideation and suicide rates are higher

© PAUL PEDROZA, 2022 | DOI:10.1163/9789004521155_006

on average for those with BPD in general, but men with BPD in particular are at risk because men are much more likely to die by suicide since we typically employ more lethal means than women.

•
• •

When I moved to Champaign, Illinois in 2006, I found myself living in a predominantly white city for the first time. I had no delusion that I would suddenly be recognized as anything but white or maybe passing—the eyebrows often rise when my last name is spoken—and I wasn't wrong. I was now a *not one of them*, no longer a *not one of us*. My name and my complexion—there was something off; the equation didn't compute.

Something that should feel so mundane, a little something to share with no real baggage, became a burden during my middle school years. The school I attended from grades sixth through eighth is located in the central area of El Paso, an area with a Mexican-American population that's a bit higher than the neighborhood where my elementary school was located. More than that, hormone levels were rising, and the halls and fields were constant proving grounds for the boys. I wasn't allowed to be invisible. They mocked my weight and my complexion almost daily. It seems that, no matter where I go, I'll never be allowed to carry half of my heritage with me.

In Champaign, I worked for a now-bankrupt bookstore chain while waiting to hear about my application for an MFA in fiction program. The bookstore's staff make up was probably typical: a good number of students of all sorts of disciplines, some lifers who really understood the bookselling business and were friendly and generous with their advice, and, of course, readers. There were a number of hopeful writers, as well. It was a mixed bag reception I received when I shared the news of my acceptance with the crew. The general manager had a good news corkboard nailed up beside the weekly schedule, and though I was hesitant to do it, I chose to share a short note instead of word of mouth, mostly to make it easier on me but also for a bit of bragging.

When I later shared some news about being accepted into a grad school prep program that helped students of underrepresented minority groups acclimate to their new environment with a white male co-worker, he asked what kind of game I was playing. I had to spend time explaining my background and the fact that the department was responsible for applying for the program for me, and I had no input in the process. It didn't seem to convince him, and it would only be the start. When I entered the program, I was immediately labeled as The Mexican, but not because I was finally "gifted" my own heritage, but because those who made their comments also wondered what kind of game I was playing. I was called a faux Mexican by one of the few students of color in the program, one of Mexican descent like me.

The comments, coming from out of nowhere made me feel like I'd stepped into a minefield from the moment I started, because I didn't expect them in a formal graduate program in an institution of higher education. They pressed buttons I wouldn't understand for years, and one reaction I had was to embrace my Mexicanness as much as I could, to flaunt it along with my unreliable Spanish. One day, on a phone call in the office of the program's literary magazine with the native Spanish-speaking husband of my partner's fellow counseling psych student, I tried to carry the whole conversation about seeing a pro-wrestling event with other friends at their apartment entirely in Spanish just to show someone something. The words were heavy on my tongue, and those that somehow crawled over and slid around the barbed barriers of my anxious mind, well ... It didn't turn out well. I was just so nervous.

I felt all of it. I told myself that if they were going to deny, deny, deny, if they thought they had the power to void, then I was going all in. I used untranslated Spanish in my stories for workshop and then sat back and listened as someone here and there struggled to get the meaning (which was always right there in the context, anyway). From time to time, I'd even ask, with sarcasm staining my terse words, if they thought I paid for this last name of mine. I felt like if I focused hard enough, I could shoot a flaming Aztec eagle through my chest, while weeping over Vicente Fernandez ballads and eating the hottest chile just because. Just to make a fucking point.

It felt like a fight. It felt like a foundation. But as soon as my partner and I left Illinois for Virginia, to spend a year in isolation save for Carol and the co-workers with whom I didn't socialize, it all dissipated like the rare desert fog of winter. It didn't feel a true part of me, nothing foundational or like a fight, about as temporary as my interest in marine biology in the sixth grade. There was no one to rage against anymore, so, like so many here-today-gone-tomorrow interests and false starts of identity, it just fell away.

• •
•

An unstable sense of self, as a symptom, might not seem so serious on the surface. You may jump from plan to plan, excited for hours, days, maybe even weeks before you lose interest and move on. You might wear different masks for the different people with whom you socialize, never taking a secure stand on beliefs and positions. When you may also be dealing with emotion regulation issues, dissociation, and suicidal ideation or non-suicidal self-harming actions, it might even seem trivial.

Over the years, after feeling convinced that certain activities, certain career options, were going to save me from feeling inadequate or from wasting my time only to lose interest, sometimes immediately, I'm convinced that it can be the symptom from which others gain their foothold. If you don't know who you are and if your efforts seem or actually are wasted, then you grow more and more unstable. This flavor of instability can bring about a good deal of suffering, and when it moves beyond the personal into the community, then all it brings is disconnect and resentment.

. .
.

The doors were still locked, and the recessed area had filled with waiting students. The day was bright and hot, a good one to spend some time in the cool library. I like to get to places early, although it's possible this experience contributed, in part, to the *likes to avoid crowds* flavor of my punctuality.

The kids crowded in, almost pressing those of us in recess against the hot steel doors. I looked through the mesh diamonds of the safety glass almost in panic, pressing back the rising dread, but the library's doors remained closed. The kids were talking about nothing in particular. The day grew hotter.

I don't remember who started it. I don't even remember if I went into the library after it finally opened or just skulked away, though I know I never visited again unless I had to for a class, the love I had for my alone time there and the books that took me away for twenty minutes at a time not strong enough to resist the shame. All I know is that the circle closed in, and there was no escape because they wouldn't allow it. Someone called me a fat fuck, or that's my best guess because I heard it all the time then, and then the chorus rose. Fucking white boy! Fuck you, you fat fucking cracker! How many lunches did you eat, pinche comelón! (Growing up, Spanish transformed from the lovely chatter of my grandparents when they spoke to my dad, aunts, and uncles into a grating, grinding nightmare that took me years to get over thanks to incidents like this.)

I doubt I said a word. Timid and anxious in those days anyway, I wasn't prepared for a surrounding mass of braying kids lobbing insults at me without provocation, so what could I have said? A realistic estimate of twelve kids still feels like dozens of dozens in the moment. I remember the eyes, the gaping laughing mouths, the pointing fingers and the hands grabbing at my chest, like exclamation points on their insults. Hey, what size bra do you wear, fat fuck?

The same thing happened during my seventh-grade year—only that time, it happened in a classroom as the teacher stood there and did nothing. In time, the insults spliced together, and when one would come, I'd wait for the other, *fatwhitefuck*. As a defense, I began to disassociate and dissociate (criterion number nine). I'd wander alone, walking up and down dirt slopes near the basketball courts where so few hung out in the morning, and I'd daydream before classes started. It calmed me, and it was better than always engaging in self-harming thoughts and behaviors (criterion number five). To this day, I still experience dissociative moments.

I *felt like* I didn't belong. I *believed* I didn't. I wasn't like anyone else, and being one of a few students of my size didn't help. Had things not been so bad at home, I might've had some species of fortitude to withstand the talk, but it'd be a while yet before I refused to go to my dad's house on weekends anymore. (It wasn't any one spectacular event. It was more like a running tab of his constant drinking and physical abuse that finally had to be called. I'm happy to share that he gave up alcohol about eighteen years ago and is a much different man when sober.) I believe one of the strongest contributors to BPD is the feeling that you don't have a space for peace, a place to go where you can shut out the torment for a while, somewhere you can mute the words and blur the faces and relax.

∵

When I come across conversations about diversity and inclusion, I usually feel that chip on my shoulder gain some weight, coloring all the possible things I could say to contribute, the shades and angles I can point out. After so many years have passed, the pain isn't so fresh, not always, but trauma never disappears. If you're lucky, it can fade, sometimes significantly, until a stray word, a nudge, sometimes something as innocuous as a scent or sound casts a harsh light, bringing out its contours once again. And I want to say something about it, but usually the words feel as heavy as that chip, and I don't know how to word it, and the moment passes.

It's not about fitting in or honoring someone's ridiculous ideal of what you're supposed to be. It's not about passing, as some have congratulated me for over the years, like it's a Get Out of Jail Free card. It's not even about fulfilling some role as cultural representative. It's about learning how to feel comfortable in one's own skin, one's unique embodiment of all that came before and helped create who you are. I've been the fat kid no one wanted to befriend, the class clown acting out because he didn't feel comfortable with himself, the guy who feels slight criticisms far too deeply at times and descends into anger first and then depression, and somehow even the token Mexican. I've felt invisible and unheard, certainly misunderstood. And in the end, what I've learned through it all, especially now that my particular experience has been given a name, is that one-dimensional, prejudicial sketches of who someone is and could be are shortsighted and lazy. They're far too easy for our complicated world. Some of us are tall and thin, some not so much. Some of us love our families whether the road has been difficult, while others' histories are thorny and deserve silence and respect. Some speak the language while others choose not to. There are no templates. When we expect them, we risk misunderstanding, division, even violence.

∴

After that day outside the library, I spent the latter halves of my lunch breaks across campus for a while. I stood in the breezeway outside the building where my next class would be held, just standing there, trying not to move too much. I'd lose myself again in those daydreams, the rock star, the quarterback, or the guy who saves the girl I was crushing on at the moment, swooping in and pushing back those who'd hurt her, but in the world too afraid to make eye contact and be devastated again. There was a group of boys there sometimes, and sometimes we'd talk about video games or TV or whatever.

Until one day, the one day that always came. That particular one day, one of the boys, himself heavier than average, stared hard at my X-Men t-shirt. There was a large red and yellow X on my chest, and his staring there made me uncomfortable, and I tried to somehow hide myself behind my crossed arms. Then, the inevitable question came. "Is that where helicopters land?" While his friends laughed and added their own jokes, I tried not to crumble, still stood there like I poured the concrete myself and stepped in. The next day, I found another place to wait out my time, and though I don't remember where, it had to have been even closer to the edges of campus.

I wonder now what he'd meant to do. At the time, I *knew* he meant to hurt me, but now, I'm not sure. They'd been friendly before that, so maybe it was meant as a joke, but for me, there was too much baggage to lug around, there was no room for anything more, and it was just easier to bear when I kept to myself.

∴

My partner Carol and I returned to El Paso in 2012, the year of supposed Mayan apocalypse. It was anything but.

I was ready for a return after a difficult year in Virginia, and I was lucky enough to make a return to teaching, where I was afforded opportunities, here and there, to teach university-level creative writing classes on the border, something I wanted to do since I took classes in creative writing as an undergrad on the border. My mental health was, of course, still a concern, but empowered with the names of my particular issues, I felt ready to move forward. A place that once might have seemed antagonistic to a confused and wounded kid offered, upon return, a chance for healing in many different shades.

I've always seen my home city as a geographical representation of the concept I now have a name for, this unstable sense of self. Caught between cultures, not developed strictly out of one or the other, but of a synergy of both that can warp and shift without notice, the El Paso-Juárez metropolitan area is as complicated as its history suggests it should be. Now, though, it's a comfort. It shows me how beauty and complexity can emerge from disparate influences, how a foundation can exist even when things seem to be changing by the moment.

I've grown comfortable with my ambivalence over my identity, as it relates to those things I have no control over, my genetics and my heritage. There are no easy answers for many of us, hence why escapism is such a temptation. For people like me, those with BPD or similar diagnoses, the stakes are a little higher. For a writer with BPD, one who publishes and attends conferences and such, well, they're just a bit higher still. The best I can do is recognize my limitations and my progress, see the path still laid out in front of me, and step forward, like that kid promised himself he'd do once he'd learned how to swim the oceans.

CHAPTER 6

Regresando a Casa

Jumko Ogata-Aguilar

Abro la puerta del Versa negro y me asomo para preguntar:

—Hola, ¿Jorge de Uber?

—Sí, buenas tardes.

Subo al auto y después de corroborar mi destino decido hacerle plática al chofer porque estaremos al menos cuarenta minutos en el viaje. Que si el clima, el tráfico, conversaciones sobre nada en particular. Hablamos de comida cuando me doy cuenta que dice "Burger King" con una pronunciación muy similar a la mía.

—Estuviste del otro lado, ¿verdad?

—Sí, ... ¿cómo te diste cuenta?

Jorge vacila antes de contestar y reconozco su reacción incómoda. Tal vez cree que le voy a preguntar si es extranjero, así que contesto rápidamente:

—Yo estuve en California ¿y tú?

Veo a través del retrovisor que sonríe—yo también me siento muy contenta al encontrar a otro chicano acá en la ciudad.

—Florida, al norte de Miami.

Enseguida empezamos a hablar en la mezcla de español e inglés que nos es tan habitual, fluyendo de una lengua a otra entre oraciones y palabras mexicanas o estadounidenses.

Hablamos de la vida allá, el cambio al regresar, cómo nos tuvimos que adaptar de nuevo.

—*Shark*. Siempre me molestaban con esa palabra, no la podía recordar. Hasta me empezaron a decir así, "el tiburón". Ahora no se me olvida. Tiburón. Ti-bu-rón.

Apenas lleva un año y medio aquí, y aún no se ha acostumbrado del todo.

—*Adapt and conquer, that's my motto when I got here, y'know? The bad thing is that it hasn't worked out that great* ...

Sus historias me hacen recordar mis primeros años después de regresar a México. Sí, es difícil hablar todo el tiempo en español, aprender con el *shock* cultural cómo relacionarte con los demás, y en especial, sentir que a pesar de haber regresado a casa, seguimos siendo extranjeros.

Me cuenta que está en la universidad, aprovechando que la educación es barata, y se compró un coche para trabajar los fines de semana de chofer. Dice

© JUMKO OGATA-AGUILAR, 2022 | DOI:10.1163/9789004521155_007

que casi no tiene amigos en la escuela, porque son mucho menores que él, y sus temas de conversación lo aburren. Quiere adoptar un perro (un pastor alemán, para ser preciso) pero esta ciudad, y el poco espacio de su departamento compartido lo detienen.

—*Yeah, back home I had a yard, I got it fenced so that the dogs could run around, be wild and all that.* Mi roomie tiene un bulldog, lo saca dos veces al día, media hora en la mañana y media hora en la tarde. Pero siento que no es suficiente, los perros necesitan más.

Asiento con la cabeza y le digo que pienso lo mismo.

Estudia ingeniería eléctrica en la UAM y me enseña orgulloso su credencial.

—*It was international relations or this, back home I used to work with these kinds of things, I really like pulling things apart and putting them back together, so I'm already pretty used to this.*

Dice que no le va del todo bien en la escuela porque tiene dificultades para mantener su promedio, aunque estudia y entrega sus tareas.

—Mi hermano cree que es por el idioma, me dijo que no sea tan duro conmigo mismo, que le de tiempo.

—¿Y tú crees que sea eso?

—No ... no realmente ... *you know, that's the thing with math ... it's always the same, no matter the language.* Él sí nació allá, mi hermano. *I was born in* Michoacán. Pero llegamos a Florida cuando yo tenía tres años, *so I've never known anything else.* Los de migración me dijeron que me tenía que regresar ... y pues me vine, llegué con mi familia a Michoacán pero decidí mudarme acá porque hay más más oportunidades. *I won't be able to go back for ten years.* No voy a poder ver a mi hermano, a mis papás, a mis perros, a mis amigos, hasta dentro de diez años. Pero pues ... ya llevo uno ... ya falta menos.

Y se ríe, deshaciéndose del temblor que se apoderó por un instante de su voz. Yo finjo no haberme dado cuenta y mejor cambio de tema.

—Pero mira, tienes que hacer amigos ... tienes que tener a quién hablarle cuando se te ponche una llanta en un barrio que no conoces o cuando te enfermes ... alguien que te ayude cuando lo necesites.

—*Yeah, you're right. I'm gonna try.* Oye ... ¿no tienes hambre? Yo no he comido y pues, nomás me voy a comprar algo de comida rápida y sigo trabajando. Si tú tampoco has comido, pues podemos pasar por algo y comer ahí en el estacionamiento. Y de ahí te llevo a tu casa, pero como tú quieras, no quiero incomodarte.

No estoy segura de qué responder, se ve amable pero ya he escuchado tantísimas historias de mujeres que se suben a un Uber para nunca más aparecer que siento ansiedad y no sé si confiar en él. Ya estamos a un par de cuadras de mi casa y recuerdo que por aquí hay una pizzería ... igual si no me da buena espina fácilmente me puedo meter al metro o irme caminando a casa.

—Pues, va. Mira, aquí adelante está la pizzería, aquí mismo estaciónate.

Jorge detiene el carro en la entrada, termina mi viaje en la aplicación y apaga el motor.

—¿Qué sabor quieres?

—El que sea, tú elige.

—*Does pepperoni sound good?*

—*Sure.*

Jorge regresa con la caja de cartón y yo me paso al asiento delantero, dejando la puerta bien abierta por si acaso. El estacionamiento está lleno, y muchas personas también están en sus carros comiendo, así que me siento más tranquila. Nos pasamos la caja de pizza y comemos en lo que hablamos sobre la vida en la Ciudad de México.

Al terminar, me pregunta si quiero llevarme algunas rebanadas a casa.

—*For dinner, want some?*

—No, no te preocupes, te lo agradezco mucho.

—Órale, la guardo entonces.

Se baja a meter la caja de pizza a la cajuela y regresa al asiento del piloto.

—Bueno, ya te llevo, ¿va? Tú me dices por dónde.

—*Thanks,* ya es aquí cerca.

Entra por el par de calles que llevan a mi casa y se detiene en el lugar que le indiqué. De cualquier manera me bajé un par de casas antes de la mía, sólo por si acaso.

Se apodera de mí una cierta tristeza, quisiera poder continuar la conversación que llevamos, porque tiene mucho que no hablo con otro chicano.

—*Good luck, man.* Todo va a funcionar, vas a ver.

—Gracias, yo espero que sí. Ah, mira, si alguna vez llegas a necesitar ...

Saca de su bolsillo una tarjeta con su número y me la pasa.

Servicio de transporte ejecutivo

—También doy clases de inglés, por si llegas a saber de alguien que necesite.

Sonrío y la guardo en mi bolsa.

—Gracias, por todo. De verdad.

Me bajo del auto y me quedo observando hasta que arranca.

Ojalá le vaya bien, espero que le vaya muy bien.

Veo cómo da vuelta a la esquina y desaparece en las fauces de la ciudad.

CHAPTER 7

我，外国女人，"Me, Foreign Woman"

Andrea Gómez

I don't remember going through Customs or checking in my luggage. I only have the vivid feeling of my left hand being slowly crushed by my mother's grip, while hearing my flight number being called on the speaker. I got my hand out of hers and ran towards the boarding gate, away from everybody and everything I had known before.

In my head, my future in France was going to be bright and peaceful. This plane was taking me to a destiny where nobody could hurt me. Little did I know it was going to be the last day I would put feet down in my home country. Of course, my assumptions were extremely naïve and it took barely four days to realize it. The mockery about my accent. The disdain when the counter lady saw my face. The jokes about students being "exotic" instead of intelligent. So, very quickly I understood this utopia of France I had built in my head was very far from reality. However, I still did not quite get why my idealization of this western world had become so strong, even to the extreme of crossing an ocean to grasp it. Partly, I stayed a couple of years there to explore these reasons. Also, I did not have anywhere else to go.

When I was five years old, I began studying at a private school. Before my admission, I had visited a few other places, and once I took an aptitude test. The institution was chosen because it was located in a wealthy neighbourhood, but taunted as a "new rich" enclave. Therefore, my family's hope was that it would be easier for me to form social, profitable connections. In addition, this school taught English and French beginning in primary school. During my time there, my family, my teachers and even random people hearing me revising these languages would reinforce the same idea.

You keep studying and you will not be poor anymore. Europe is better. The US is great. Go. Those *blanquitos*[1] are not like us. Go. Don't waste your opportunities. Go.

∵

I left France to go, as an exchange student, to Brazil. It was one of the best years of my life. Finally, I could get out of my house and not be discriminated against.

© ANDREA GÓMEZ, 2022 | DOI:10.1163/9789004521155_008

People were charming and treated me with respect. With very few exceptions, living there was like a breath of fresh air.

A fellow student from my university e-mailed me during this time. She wanted to choose the same location for an internship, but isn't it very poor and dangerous in São Paulo? I chuckled. Look, poverty is global. This country is almost as big as a continent. Of course, there are poor people, and there are rich people, as well. Poverty won't attack you. I recalled various micro-aggressions and a couple of overt attacks towards me in the supposedly developed nation she was still living in, and yet only the single attempt of pickpocketing I faced in Brazil. You will be ok, my response concluded. Never heard from her again.

Occasionally, it was pointed out to me that I was not afraid of visiting the city quarters deigned "epicentres of crime" by the local media. I would answer sharing stories about my childhood. In Europe, I didn't technically study at a university. I went to a *grand école*. People assumed I had come from wealth, or at least from an upper-class household. After I told them I once ate one quarter of a baked potato for a whole day, and that I lived in a house 10 blocks from the city's penitentiary, and without working drainage, their faces would change.

With time, my life became one of a traveller, and I am currently living in yet another foreign country. Nevertheless, my familiarity with crossing into unknown territories dates from decades ago; when I was also chasing the promise of education but for the mere purpose of just surviving.

When I was five years old, I crossed my first border. A geographically defined, social class border.

∴

A national TV station used to make history specials, and one of them was about Peruvian anthropologist and writer José María Arguedas. He still represents a fiercely and proudly Andean literature, deeply rooted in the racist and oligarchical realities lived in the rural areas of Peru. Arguedas wrote in Spanish while his prose came from Quechua.

During the programme, his debate with novelist Julio Cortázar was mentioned. When the latter argued Latin American writers should move away from "provincial" complexes, and that it is sometimes necessary for them to be far from their own countries of origin to comprehend local and national realities, Arguedas answered. From his response comes his well-known retort: "*Todos somos provincianos don Julio [Cortázar]. Provincianos de las naciones y provincianos de lo supranacional*" (Arguedas, 1971).[2]

While I was listening to this discussion, its impact on literature seemed irrelevant. I was fifteen, going through the end of a dictatorship, and frantically looking for college options abroad. During my brief life, I had experienced my hometown of Lima as a multitude of cities. Its economic and social disparities can only be ignored if there is a permanent intent of not leaving its tacit frontiers. Did Cortázar never go through Buenos Aires or Paris and visit all of its extremes? What is so wrong with being provincial, or did he mean something else?

On the horizon, another constraint sets loose. The land of my ancestor, whose transatlantic journey has been my inspiration since adolescence. The fluidity and uneasiness of the borders around us defy our lives constantly. I have chosen to embrace it, rejoicing in its uncertainty. Go. Without preconceptions. Go. Always remembering where you come from. Go. To another continent, or around the block. Go.

Notes

1   Spanish word that translates to *"whiteys."* In this case, it was used as an endearment term.
2   Original quote in Spanish: "We are all provincial Don Julio [Cortázar]. Provincials of the nations and provincials of the supranational" (Arguedas, 1971).

Reference

Arguedas, J. M. (1971). *El zorro de arriba y el zorro de abajo*. Editorial Losada.

CHAPTER 8

Liminality

Rachel Neff

1. Liminal is a three-syllable adjective meaning "of or relating to a transitional or initial stage of process" or "occupying a position at, or on both sides of, a boundary or threshold" (Toscano, 2016).
2. I could have been born on August 15, but my mom was tired from working her nursing shift, and she told the doctor she'd come back the next day.
3. A liminal being cannot easily be placed in a single category. Examples include centaurs, the Sphinx, Caliban, and cyborgs.
4. Walking past me at lunch he sneered "It ain't right for a woman to read so much," as I sat on the floor in front of the door to my high school Spanish class.
5. In Greek mythology, a chimera was a female creature with a lion's head, goat's body, and serpent's tail. Fierce, independent, and phallic. Even without the animal body parts, some might consider a woman with those traits to be monstrous.
6. The *Oxford English Dictionary* first defines the adjective queer as "strange, odd, peculiar, eccentric." It continues "Also: of questionable character; suspicious, dubious." First example in a text composed circa 1513.
7. The first known use of the term "snake oil" was in 1927 in a poem titled *John Brown's Body*.
8. In graduate school, between doing archival research on Maria Reina Rodríguez at Princeton's Firestone Library and visiting my aunt in New York City, I decided to buy a knockoff bag. My mom's friend had asked me to pick her up an imitation Coach handbag. My finder's fee was enough to buy a bag for myself. Scoping out the best deal and selection, I ended up on Canal Street negotiating and walking away when I knew the price was too high. One vendor and I locked eyes, both knowing what was fair – the fun was in the haggling. I reached for the bag that I wanted and was testing the zippers when a man ducked in to her stall and started speaking in a foreign language. They began to yank down sheets to hide the merchandise, all except the boxy, black and white satchel in my hands. The man opened a door in the back of the stall and stepped inside. The woman pushed me (and the bag) in there with him and shut the door. There we were, in a space the size of a closet. We stood there, silent, breathing. He reached

up, grabbed the chain and yanked. Darkness. Footsteps. His breath against my neck. Would I still be an innocent buyer if the police served a warrant and found us together in the dark, me sweating and clutching the plastic forgery to my chest as a barrier between him and me?

9. *Merriam-Webster*'s first definition for the adjective queer is "worthless, counterfeit." The first known use of the adjective was in 1508.

10. My first spelling bee was on a weekend in a school somewhere. I sat at a desk where my feet swung between rounds. My dad walked me into a brick building where I misspelled "gown" in classroom 215.

11. In the third grade, my penchant for acquiring new vocabulary words, replete with definitions, earned me the nickname "Walking, Talking Dictionary." It was not meant as a compliment.

12. In fifth grade, I paused too long and then restarted on the l, going out on "celery." I didn't enter any spelling bees after elementary school. I've never misspelled gown or celery since either.

13. First known use of the verb and noun "queer," according to *Merriam-Webster*: 1812.

14. The letter R comes after Q in the alphabet. You could also say Q comes before R. Add a few vowels in between and perhaps we begin to understand and approach an identity.

15. My favorite letter is R. It's one of the first I learned how to write. A straight line, followed by a curve starting at the top of the line, ending near the middle. Then comes the hard part, where to place the angled line to change the P to an R. When learning how to print, no shortcuts were allowed. The pencil had to be lifted and repositioned. No cheating. The third line of the letter R had to perfectly bisect the loop. It couldn't start at the end of the loop. Once you learn to print, you learn it is faster to connect the leg to the loop, which you are allowed to do with cursive, something I wouldn't learn for several more years. An early lesson in the system's ideal versus real. The way things are versus the way we say they should be.

16. I often think in a mix of English and Spanish. I've been mistaken for an Argentine, Spaniard, and a Mexican.

17. People see me and want to know where I learned the language.

18. I once invited a classmate over for a *polvo* sandwich instead of *pavo*. Dust, turkey, it was close enough, right?

19. The second definition for the adjective queer in *Merriam-Webster* is "differing in some odd way from what is usual or normal; eccentric, unconventional: mildly insane: touched; absorbed or interested to an extreme or unreasonable degree: obsessed; *often disparaging* : homosexual."

20. "You're not one of them weird ones that likes girls, are you?" my cousin asked while we played pool. He asked the question because I was in middle school and didn't have a boyfriend.

21. I read an article published in *Slate* where the author, Mario Vittone, wrote "Drowning is almost always a deceptively quiet event." Even the title stuck with me, "Drowning Doesn't Look Like Drowning." He goes on to detail a person's Instinctive Drowning Response, which doesn't match the splashing and screaming we see in the movies and on TV. In fact, most drowning victims can't speak because their bodies are so focused on trying to breathe that speech is suppressed. Those screaming for help are in distress, but not yet drowning.

22. I woke up thinking "Every day I wake up and I haven't died in my sleep is a terrible day." Then I had to go to work.

23. My first panic attack happened when I was in the waiting room of the student health clinic. My appointment was at 1:15 p.m. and the nurse practitioner was supposed to give me the results of the colposcopy. I remember looking at the man to my right, wanting him to offer me his hand to hold. The world felt cold and small. I was taken back to the exam room and the clock kept going forward and forward, but the nurse did not appear. It was 1:45 p.m. I concluded the only reason for this kind of delay was that she had bad news.

24. The third *Merriam-Webster* definition for the adjective queer is "not quite well."

25. The Mayo Clinic defines Hashimoto's disease as "a condition in which your immune system attacks your thyroid, a small gland at the base of your neck below your Adam's apple."

26. I tell the nurses at the student health clinic I feel tired. Every single one assumes it's because I'm up late studying. I try to go to bed at 8 p.m., but my mind races and I find myself bolting upright and screaming for no reason around 2 a.m. I drag myself out of bed to teach my 8 a.m. class. It's the kind of tired that makes you think that Hamlet's version of sleeping might be the solution to the numb exhaustion and constant anxiety.

27. Cedars-Sinai explains that Hashimoto's thyroiditis patients are more likely to experience fatigue; drowsiness; forgetfulness; dry, brittle hair and nails; dry, itchy skin; puffy face; constipation, sore muscles; weight gain; heavy menstrual flow; and increased sensitivity to many medications.

28. My face is so swollen people start to congratulate me on the baby. My voice becomes huskier. A friend (then enemy then friend again) says, "I always thought you looked like a tranny."

29. In 1972, the *OED* quotes P.A. Bastenie and A.M. Ermans' *Thyroiditis & Thyroid Function* v. 110 "The progress of untreated Hashimoto's thyroiditis is variable."

30. I kept asking the psychiatrist and student health center doctors about ruling out Hashimoto's. They said the tests said no.

31. In the *OED*, the second definition for the adjective queer is "Out of sorts; unwell; faint, giddy." First usage 1749.

32. It took three months and nodules in my thyroid that needed to be biopsied after the ultrasound showed them to be concerning for me to see an endocrinologist who accepted my student health insurance. He ran three tests. "Yep, it's Hashimoto's." The student clinic doctors were looking for signs of a dead thyroid, not a dying one.

33. ICD.Codes.com quotes Wikipedia as saying "Hashimoto's thyroiditis or chronic lymphocytic thyroiditis is an autoimmune disease in which the thyroid gland is attacked by a variety of cell- and antibody-mediated immune processes."

34. The endocrinologist in Texas feels my neck and says "Classic Hashimoto's thyroid." He makes the medical student feel it so she, too, knows how a classic case should feel when palpated.

35. I become a pincushion every six weeks while the endocrinologist works out the right dose of synthroid, but synthroid is one of the few medications where "do not substitute for generic" really matters. I don't want to ask my parents for help with the co-pays, so I get the generic. Some months, I drop ten pounds, other months, the weight comes right back.

36. I start searching the Internet for any and all kinds of home remedies. I sob because I'm desperate to feel anything other than achy, tired, and miserable that the snake-oil salesmen of the digital age are offering me as hope.

37. The third *OED* entry for queer is "Of a person: homosexual. Hence: of or relating to homosexuals or homosexuality."

38. My first sex dream is about my best friend. I wake up pulsating and shivering, and I know it's something I can never tell her.

39. A chimera can also be "a thing that is hoped or wished for but in fact is illusory or impossible to achieve."

40. "There's no such thing as bisexuality," one lover told me. I got tired of his drinking after a month and stopped returning his calls.

41. According to Wikipedia, "In anthropology, liminality (from the Latin word līmen, meaning 'a threshold') is the quality of ambiguity or disorientation that occurs in the middle stage of rituals, when participants no longer hold their pre-ritual status but have not yet begun the transition to the status they will hold when the ritual is complete."

42. At staff yoga, I go to repeat downward dog, and I feel funny. I go to child's pose to rest, but the feeling of cold sweat and nausea continues. The walk back to the office is hazy. A coworker drives me to the urgent care. The EKG suggests an enlarged left ventricle. I call home. "What's wrong?" my mother asks.

43. One of the possible complications of Hashimoto's is heart failure. At 28, I had a cardiologist. I spent more on medical bills in a year than most people put on down payments for cars.

44. What happens when what you thought you would be does not match the reality?

45. These are bits of memory that tumble out, that I blow off the dust to examine. I am becoming who I was always meant to be.

References

Benét, S. V. (2007, April). *John Brown's body*. Project Gutenberg Australia. http://gutenberg.net.au/ebooks07/0700461.txt

Cedars-Sinai. (2021). *Hashimoto thyroiditis*. Cedars. https://www.cedars-sinai.org/health-library/diseases-and-conditions/h/hashimotos-thyroiditis.html

Chimaera. (2021). In *A grammatical dictionary of botanical Latin*. https://www.mobot.org/mobot/latindict/keyDetail.aspx?keyWord=chimaera

ICD. Codes. (2021). *ICD-10-CM Code E06.3 Autoimmune thyroiditis*. ICD. Codes – The Medical Coding Resource. https://icd.codes/icd10cm/E063

Mayo Clinic. (2020, February 11). *Hashimoto's disease*. Mayo Foundation for Medical Education and Research. https://www.mayoclinic.org/diseases-conditions/hashimotos-disease/symptoms-causes/syc-20351855

Merriam-Webster. (n.d.). *Queer*. Merriam-Webster. https://www.merriam-webster.com/dictionary/queer

Oxford English dictionary. (1989). Oxford University Press. https://www.oed.com/oed2/00194686;jsessionid=29800D0408C3B2E9D6BF3ACB049B00E7

Toscano, P. (2016). *In between people and in between spaces*. Retreat Leader for Foundry UMC LGBTQ Retreat (Rehoboth Beach). https://petersontoscano.com/events/event/retreat-leader-for-foundry-umc-lgbtq-retreat-rehoboth-beach/

Vittone, M. (2013, June 4). Drowning doesn't look like drowning. *Slate Magazine*. https://slate.com/technology/2013/06/rescuing-drowning-children-how-to-know-when-someone-is-in-trouble-in-the-water.html

Wikimedia Foundation. (2021, April 15). Liminality. In *Wikipedia*. https://en.wikipedia.org/wiki/Liminality

CHAPTER 9

Las Guardianas de la Identidad

Two Poems

Ana Silvia Monzón Monterroso

I.

Digo que soy feminista
y de todas las religiones se santiguan
rezan, oran o maldicen
sacan su catecismo de "ideología de género"
y me echan agua bendita

Digo que soy feminista
¡burguesa! ¡imperialista!
dicen los comunistas
Y todo el espectro de las izquierdas progresistas
tradicionales, con línea, sin línea, o anarquistas

Digo que soy feminista
¡racista, etnocéntrica, occidental!
dicen desde el *mainstream* decolonial
(del cual soy crítica devota)
porque lo patriarcal
-dicen-
siempre viene después de lo colonial
nunca antes, cuando todo era virginal
puro y esencial

digo que soy feminista
demasiado hetero
dicen desde la diversidad sexual
no nos gustan las etiquetas
dicen desde las tribus queer/inter/trans
porque aquí las identidades son líquidas
dependen del humor matinal

© ANA SILVIA MONZÓN MONTERROSO, 2022 | DOI:10.1163/9789004521155_010

digo que soy feminista
egocéntrica, individualista
sin sentido de la colectividad
dicen ¡a coro! todos los movimientos

digo que soy feminista
sesgada, acientífica
dicen los sesudos intelectuales puristas
estridente
dicen los muy ecuánimes dirigentes

digo que soy feminista
y me voy quedando sola
como la Eva que comió del fruto prohibido
como Hypatia en Alejandría
como la Virgen María y María Magdalena
revolucionarias pero distorsionadas
como Ixquic acusada de deshonra
como la Malinche repudiada
como Sor Juana en el claustro
frente al obispo
como Olympia frente al cadalso
como Mary frente a Rosseau
como Clara frente a Lenin
como Simone frente a Sartre
como Angela frente a Los Panteras
como las Mirabal frente a sus verdugos
como Mayra frente a sus secuestradores
como Berta frente a sus asesinos
como Marielle frente a los sicarios
como cada una que se preguntó
¿qué es ser mujer?
¿qué es ser feminista?

ii. Mestizas

Mujeres
demasiado blancas
para los estándares indígenas

demasiado morenas
para los estándares de las blancas
les falta "color"
para los estándares de las afrodescendientes
¿les falta algo para ser humanas?
Se les niega historia
Se les niega identidad
se les acusa de falta de linaje
¿dónde están sus orígenes?
¿dónde la prueba de su humanidad?
marcadas por el rechazo de la madre indígena
violada
negadas por el padre invasor
síntesis de dos o varios mundos
sobrevivientes de la hostilidad
señaladas de fragilidad
inculpadas de ambigüedad
¿Dónde están sus raíces?
¿dónde su tronco común?
preguntan desde su pedestal de pureza
las guardianas de la identidad

PART 3

Thin Edge of Barbwire

∵

CHAPTER 10

Welcome to Colonia Libertad

Jorge Omar Ramírez Pimienta

Welcome to Colonia Libertad

"Collapsing Liberty" aims to generate a visual representation of deportation by tracing a relationship between political iconography and human displacement. The piece expands from *Welcome to Colonia Libertad*, an extended project that examines one of Tijuana's oldest neighborhoods, it's long historical relationship with migration since its foundation in 1929, and its rapid occupation by repatriated Mexicans from the great depression of the 1930's. The piece collapses and inflates. Each collapse represents 10,000 deportees. Each hour correlates to a specific year in the presidential term of Barak Obama.

FIGURE 10.1 Collapsing Liberty by Jorge Omar Ramírez Pimienta (http://omarpimienta.com/collapsing-liberty/)

FIGURE 10.2   Cosulado Movil/Mobile Consulate. Portraiture of applicants that undergo
a bureaucratic action that emulates the process of acquiring a passport
(dimensions: variable; date: 2012 to date; http://omarpimienta.com/
free-citizens-only-application)

FIGURE 10.3   Archive of Free Citizens. Intervened passports traded for the Pasaporte
Libre (dimensions: variable; year: 2012–2019; http://omarpimienta.com/
consulado-movil-mobile-consulate/)

FIGURE 10.4   Lady Libertad V2. An ephemeral monument set to intervene the public space
               of Colonia Libertad (date: 2009; http://omarpimienta.com/lady-libertad-v2/)

FIGURE 10.5   Lady Libertad V1. Plaster sculpture and photographic series of apparitions
               of Lady Libertad, produced in Colonia Libertad (date: 2007–2009;
               http://omarpimienta.com/lady-v1/)

Album of Fences

FIGURE 10.6   Don Marcos at home

3.
my father's name was Prisciliano Gil Bautista (Indiana 1931–†Tijuana 1957)
my father's name is Marcos Ramírez López (Jalisco 1929)

official documents
papel picado by time
signatures: lines that travel on a roller coaster

Prisciliano Gil Bautista worked with the body:
Marcos Ramírez López

Marcos Ramírez López worked with the name:
Prisciliano Gil Bautista

Marcos bought an identity
Prisciliano donated a social organ
wrapped in papel picado

my father remembers
the last name of the immigration officer: Cruz
what's your name?

Prisciliano Gil Bautista oficial
no Prisciliano Gil Bautista está muerto

now I wonder if my father died a little in that other body.

FIGURE 10.7
Don Marcos working at his Taller de Herrería

9.
don Marcos: did you always use a baseball cap?

yes-son

what I rarely used was my head

don Marcos: how many times did you get deported?

one or two

lost track don Marcos?

my son   I lost everything.

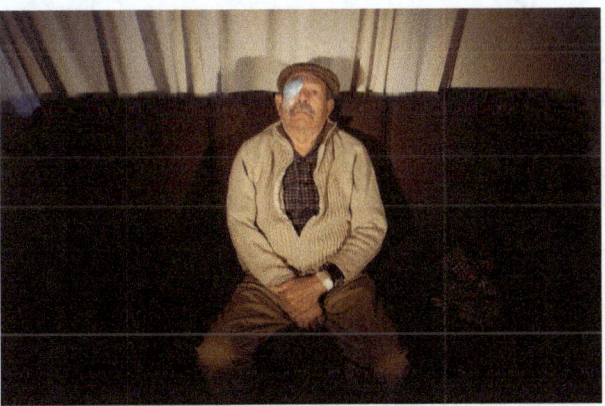

FIGURE 10.8   Don Marcos at Colonia Libertad

10.
Don Marcos
brags about never having crossed the border illegally

with fake ID s   yes

always through the gate
looking the customs officer in the eye

with a fake name yes

never through the hill
never through the desert
never through the river

I never crossed illegally never really being my self.

CHAPTER 11

Salamandra

Filiberto Mares Hernández

Salamandra, o para los amigos Sali, esperaba que esta historia no empezara dentro de un carro y en pleno sol de verano de un año llamado 2020. Sí, ajá, 2020. Pero sí, no había de otra. Había leído el cuento "La autopista del sur" de Julio Cortázar por razones del azar. Hacía tan sólo un par de días que alguien lo había compartido en su muro de Facebook. Lo leyó con agilidad como leer cualquier hilo de algo en tuiter y los chorizos de Facebook. Le molestó que su historia también sucediera ahí, frente al volante, en una fila de autos y para su causa, sudando a todo lo que daba por cada uno de sus poros. De la gasolina no se preocuparía, había llenado el tanque antes de entrar a la ciudad. La había prevenido tanto su hija Kasandra, de ya cuarenta años (no que sean muchos, pero para alguien de siete sí que lo son), tanto le había dado la cantaleta que todavía sentía su eco en la oreja.

La fila se erigía por varios kilómetros. Estaba lejos de la entrada. Muy a lo lejos algunas personas se bajaban a comprar nieve en un puestesito. La lengua, la saliva y los paladares apestosos, pareciera, eran los ganadores de la tarde. Salamandra se imaginó una tarde de agosto en una plaza de cualquier pueblo, junto a la vendedora de nieves frescas, a punto de llevarse la cucharada de nieve de limón a la boca. No dejó que la melancolía la atrapara con tanta fuerza como la atrapaba el recuerdo de unos buenos tacos al pastor en la esquina de cualquier plaza de cualquier pueblo de su país. Al sur.

Le dijo a Kasandra (nombre que se robó de una telenovela de las ocho de la noche en los años ochenta, y que por cierto, a su difunto marido nunca le gustó), hace un par de días que era más fácil leer veinte minutos de chismes en el celular que leer un cuento. Kasandra también le recalcó que esas historias de las redes sociales, o chorizos como ella les decía, que también eran buenos cuentos porque pasaban en la vida real. Que esas cosas eran chingonas y no eran tarugadas. Palabra que nunca le gustó decir, pero que su padre siempre la decía cuando quería descalificar algo. Esas sí que son tarugadas. Kasandra la heredó como algo perdurable.

A lo lejos divisó luces y una gran cerca. Su corazón se comenzó a agitar, pero no dejó que su vida se redujera a ese preciso momento. A una simple y llana pared. La vida no era una pared, y eso sí que lo sabía. Se puso un poco de rímel

© FILIBERTO MARES HERNÁNDEZ, 2022 | DOI:10.1163/9789004521155_012 en los ojos. Kasandrá se lo había regalado la navidad pasada. Bien lo recuerda, "Feliz 2020 y que todo, todo, sea tuyo", y luego un trago al tequila.

Faltaba menos para llegar a el punto donde tenía que abrir la cajuela y otras puertas, si es que fuera necesario. Bueno, nunca se sabía del carácter y humor de los trabajadores (porque ella también trabajaba atendiendo a personas). Todo dependía de los que estaban en turno. No se quiso bajar del auto como muchas personas lo comenzaban a hacer. ¿Para qué? Si todos iban para el mismo lugar. Cruzar una frontera más. Abrió el Facebook en su celular solamente para ver de inicio que alguien había puesto unas fotos de cervezas bien frías y, así, de rápido lo cerró. No se iba a torturar. Si ya la tortura era buena, para qué más.

Llegó su turno. Ya casi ni sudaba. En esperar algo sí que era buena. Había esperado tanto una vida mejor, que todo esto para Salamandra era pan comido. Se bajó del auto cuando una señora de pelo canoso le dio el sí. Recordó a su marido, no muerto con la bala de los narcos como sucedió, pero sí degustando una deliciosa nieve de lima en la plaza de su pueblito (cualquier pueblo que se imaginen). Al llegar su turno le dijo a la persona en turno, échele dos bolsas de papas, dos cajas de esas grandes, aquellas manzanas y dos galones de leche. Esta semana va a estar más cabrona.

CHAPTER 12

Corazón Fronterizo

Two Collages

Isabela Ortega

In composing "Heart of the Borderland," I chose to focus on the poem "One Art" by Elizabeth Bishop. In the poem, Bishop explores the theme of loss, progressing from mundane things such as losing your car keys to losing a loved one. On August 3rd, 2019 a gunman opened fire at a Walmart in El Paso, Texas. The assailant admitted that his actions were "in response to the Hispanic invasion of Texas." On August 7th, my mom and I visited the memorial of this shooting. This same feeling of loss and longing was prominent that day at the Walmart.

At the memorial, one can look straight ahead and see the iconic words "LA BIBLIA ES LA VERDAD LEELA" painted on the side of a mountain in the city of Juarez, Mexico. The El Paso star, a prominent symbol of the city, can also be seen in the piece. These mountains are then connected by a single heart, representing El Paso and its significance as the heart of this frontier between the United States and Mexico and the huge amount of heart that El Pasoans have, despite this tragic event that took place. On the upper canvas, pieces of the shooter's manifesto are collaged along with flowers. A hand coming from this section of the piece is reaching to take the heart that unites this boundary between two worlds. This manifesto made a massive impression on many and make it one of the most shocking parts of this event, because of its racist, anti-immigrant, white supremacist, and hatred-filled language.

∴

The word "imprecation" is defined as a curse or a wish of ill upon oneself or another person. When conducting research on this word, I couldn't help but think that the epitome of wishing ill upon someone else was demonstrated on August 3rd, 2019 at the Cielo Vista Walmart shooting in El Paso, Texas. The accompanying etchings entitled "La Rosa de El Paso" are inspired by the cards of the Mexican bingo game, "Loteria", using images that symbolize this incident and were sourced from reference photos that I took at the memorial. The star card, or "La Estrella," depicts the El Paso star that so recognizably symbolizes the city of El Paso. The hand card, or "La Mano" illustrates the weapon or

© ISABELA ORTEGA, 2022 | DOI:10.1163/9789004521155_013

FIGURE 12.1   "Heart of the Borderland (Corazón Fronterizo)" by Isabela Ortega

FIGURE 12.2   "La Rosa de El Paso" by Isabela Ortega

the "hand" that was used to cause destruction on the scene. The death card, or "La Muerte," portrays the crosses at the memorial that represent all of the 22 lives lost in the shooting. The flags card, or "Las Banderas," depicts the Mexican, American, and Texas flags that wave in the wind at the memorial.

CHAPTER 13

My Friends from Work

Fidel García Reyes

are not from around here
they came in rocket ships
swimming across tidal rivers
or walking through blazing deserts
      filled with rainbows and silky butterflies

back home,
their people know little
about loneliness
or the lack of kindness
that wall off my work friends

back there
they know little
about how lives are measured
in months
in borders
and by how fast they can save for this or that

back there
they think my friends
stay in:
don't go out or love
"it's too expensive!"
but few know that
each check is just enough
for rent and eating poorly

we send home el otro poquito
to pay for el cumpleaños de la mamá
or sleek
      secondhand trucks
      for baby brothers

my brown friends from work
with their broken English and broken visas
shelve fancy college degrees
alongside their beautiful
colorized
spirits

they learn to fly alone
navigating alien forms
ticking boxes for taxes
insurance and hospital bills
all to support a dream:
                    not *ours*
with no choice but to survive
on the edge of a solitary nervous breakdown.

CHAPTER 14

Las casas y nosotros

Verónica Gaona

Las casas y nosotros is a photographic series that explores the relationships between architecture, migration and death in the context of transnational relationships within the remittance landscapes. The photographs propose the idea that remitting and migration is performative in that the laborer constructs houses but at a distance across international borders. The photos capture the multiple sense of being in relation to identity and place experienced in migrant family histories.

In the photographs, the figure moves across remittance houses and tombstones in Valle Hermoso, Tamaulipas, a Mexican border town near the Rio Grande Valley. The figure in movement and parallel against the houses is a gesture that attempts to convey the viewer into the past, showing the decaying material as a reminder of the passage of time. Research into Gaona's family's decision to live and work in the North, building aspirations in the homeland, and end-of-life planning through interviews, building receipts, and repatriation papers is undertaken but left behind to instead make sense aesthetically. Together, the photographs explore the consequences of built architecture outliving bodies and the role of architecture as an active spatial agent challenging the linearity of distance across international borders.

FIGURE 14.1
Las casas y nosotros #1 by Verónica Gaona

FIGURE 14.2   Las casas y nosotros #2 by Verónica Gaona

FIGURE 14.3   Las casas y nosotros #3 by Verónica Gaona

FIGURE 14.4   Las casas y nosotros #4 by Verónica Gaona

FIGURE 14.5   Las casas y nosotros #5 by Verónica Gaona

CHAPTER 15

I Am Enough

Erica Reyes

Medium: Charcoal, Pastels, Polyurethane

Being a Mexican American raised in America, I often feel conflicted about my identity. More than anything I have wanted to dive into and proudly claim my Hispanic roots. However, due to my the lack in my ability to speak Spanish, and with little knowledge in traditions, I often get looked down upon within the Hispanic community for not 'Being Mexican Enough.'

Growing up in a primarily white neighborhood, I was one of three Hispanics in my class, but, of the three I was also the only full-blooded Hispanic. While I did not get raised strictly in a Mexican culture, I did not get raised in a strictly American culture either. This border identity was obvious to others, and quite often, I was outcasted by the kids in my grade because of it. I faced the greatest discrimination my Sophomore year of high school, during the 2016 elections. During this time is when I felt many turned on me for not 'Being American Enough.' I struggled with this for many years, but as I came to Millikin and found my crowd who understood, I have come to realize I am me. I am Mexican American, and I am Enough.

FIGURE 15.1 *I Am Enough*

PART 4

Shadow Beast

∵

CHAPTER 16

That's Not My Name

A Journey of Reclamation

Marisa V. Cervantes

My name is Marisa. That's *Marisa* pronounced in Spanish. Roll the "r" and extend the "i." My name is not "difficult" to pronounce. My name is not complex. It does not have any silent letters or a unique spelling. It just requires you to roll the "r" and extend the "i."

My mother gave me a name that is meant to be pronounced in Spanish. Yet, from the time I started kindergarten up until now, nearing the end of my doctorate program, I have allowed myself to accept an English pronunciation. For too many years, I have lived with the discomfort of responding to a name that is not mine. I have swallowed the urge to correct people and insist that they say my name correctly. For too many years, I have reluctantly accepted an identity I never intended to own. But not anymore. At least not in the same way.

The issue of how my name is pronounced is in many ways a small issue; one that I have been told over and over is not a big deal, something I shouldn't let bother me because it doesn't change who I am. I have been told repeatedly that I should know it's hard for some people to say. "It's not their fault they can't roll their r's." True, but it is their fault if they are unwilling to try or quick to dismiss it.

The mispronunciation of someone's name is a microaggression. The consistent refusal to try is a product and reproduction of racism. The whitewashing of one's name is violence. This thing I've been led to believe isn't a big deal has consumed me for far too long. It's been the source of an enduring internal battle, a product of my Mexican American identity, and one of the most (in)visible aspects of my life in the borderlands. I've spent years managing an internal conflict over this. How did I let it get this far? Why did I allow people to call me something that is not my name? When did I become numb to it? And the one that haunts me the most, why did I adopt it as part of my identity?

Over the years I have started to figure it out piece by piece. And in that process, I've learned to forgive myself for not recognizing my own power while, at the same time, holding myself accountable to end the harm this has caused me for so long. In hindsight, it makes total sense why I would begin to respond to a name that isn't mine. The start of my education marked the beginning

© MARISA V. CERVANTES, 2022 | DOI:10.1163/9789004521155_017

of this journey. I've come to terms with the fact that I was a child who didn't know how to speak up or defend myself, or how to correct an adult, a white teacher no less. I was surrounded by white kids who had no obligation to pronounce my name correctly, since that's what the teacher called me. While I can't remember what I felt or thought as a 6-year-old, I imagine it was a confusing experience. I want to believe that I questioned it, at least internally. That I knew something wasn't right, and I should probably tell someone. But I am certain that I also knew I needed to behave and not get in trouble. I was raised to respect the adults in my life and taught not to talk back. As a result, I learned to respond to a name that isn't mine.

Risk without Reward

I remember the day we had a substitute teacher in my eighth-grade AVID class, a class intended to support underrepresented students prepare for college. She was an older white woman who found herself standing in front of a class full of Black and Brown kids. As she was calling out attendance, she said my name in a way I had never heard it said before. "Mah-ree-sa" *What?!* Immediately, everyone in the class started laughing, and I felt my face go hot. "It's Marisa" I corrected her, mispronouncing my name the way I had learned to do years ago. I soon found out she was a trained linguist, who proceeded to tell me that I had spelled my own name wrong. She explained that if I wanted to pronounce it as Marisa then it should be spelled as Marissa, with two s's. I immediately became upset and retorted that she had no place to tell me my name was wrong. And when she stood her ground to tell me I was, I realized this was my chance. "Actually, you are right" I said, "the spelling is correct because my name is meant to be pronounced in Spanish as *Marisa,*" and as soon as I said it, a smirk appeared on her face. I continued with "but since all you white people can't seem to learn how to say it right, I've had to go by this other name." This time, my classmates had my back. "Ooh, lady, she told you!" and "yeah, how are you gonna tell her that her name is wrong? What's wrong with you?"

I felt elated. I took the risk of getting in trouble to talk back and stand up for myself. I had pointed out this woman's ignorance and let everyone know how my name is supposed to sound. I was sure this meant that my friends, Brown and Black people who were capable of properly pronouncing it, would now start using my real name. But the moment passed, and no one recognized that I wasn't only trying to correct her, but all of them who also used my English name.

Nothing changed. The rush I felt from my valiance and defiance soon disappeared. So much for trying. Look at the bright side, I told myself, at least I only have to deal with this at school.

Remorse

I wish I would have made the decision to reclaim my name when I started college. I had the perfect opportunity to introduce myself as my authentic self. No one knew me there. I wouldn't have to ask people to call me by something different. I reinvented so many parts of myself except for one of the most important markers of my identity. But I had pushed my discomfort so far down, I didn't even give it a second thought.

What I didn't realize was how this new environment would blur the lines for me. Prior to college, I had a clear separation of my two worlds. At school, I went by the English name. At home, people said my name correctly. I had no idea how much harder it would be for me to keep my two worlds separate now that I was away from my family and living on campus. Now, home and school were one in the same.

At some point, my fear of correcting people transformed into something else. Before, I felt alienated by others who didn't respect me for who I was. And now, I had reached a point of alienation within myself. I used to be afraid of calling home and accidentally using the wrong name. I imagined how awful and embarrassed I'd feel if I called my grandma's house and forgot to codeswitch. I was terrified of how my family would respond if they heard me mispronounce my own name and even worse, introduce myself that way. It's not like my family didn't know I went by an English version of my name at school, but I never referred to myself that way. In fact, I hardly ever said my own name. I avoided saying it and, for a long time, even disliked it. I often found myself wishing I had an "easier" name that didn't require an English and Spanish version.

The shame I'd internalized and the guilt I felt for allowing myself to be ashamed ate at me. How could I feel this way when I knew how much my mom loved the name she'd given me? I now cringe at the thought of it: at the fact that I let myself feel this way and how low of a point I had reached. While I didn't act on it right away, I knew that something had to change.

Reclaiming

I don't remember the exact moment when I finally decided I was done responding to a name that isn't mine. What I do remember is how much I worried about how to break the news—as if it was something that would be considered news breaking—to my friends who have become family, to the person I was dating, and all the people who knew me before I made this choice to reclaim my name. I knew it wouldn't be an immediate transition, and it would take people time to remember. But I didn't think I would receive any resistance.

When I told one person that I no longer wanted to be called the English version of my name, they refused to acknowledge my request. They said they have only known me as that and, therefore, could not say my name in Spanish; it didn't feel right to them. Imagine that.

The flat-out dismissal of my efforts to rectify the internal conflict I've had for the majority of my life, the refusal to call me by my name because it was different—no, because *they* were uncomfortable with it—took precedence over respecting my existence. In that moment, I learned that this would be harder than I thought.

If I'm being honest, I did begin to question myself and ask if it was worth it. Was I willing to sacrifice the relationships with people I cared for over something that has suddenly become a big deal to me? I weighed my options and finally reached the conclusion that I have to be okay with the possibility of losing people who are unwilling to accept my wishes. If that happens, it happens. And yes, it will be terrible, but not as bad as continuing to suppress my authentic self.

Reconciliation

My issues with my identity have shaped my life in ways that I am still learning. I am coming into my own, recognizing the trauma that white supremacy has inflicted upon me in the most personal ways, and importantly, finding myself amidst the chaos that has consumed so much of my energy. Although I sometimes still catch myself using the English pronunciation of my name, like when I buy a cup of coffee or call in my pizza order, I've gotten much better at correcting myself before the word escapes my mouth. I introduce myself as *Marisa* but sometimes will let people know that I've also gone by Marisa because of racism, the erasure of non-English languages, the pressure to assimilate, and the powerlessness that comes with being part of a minoritized community in this country. I can always tell who in the room gets it, from the small smiles that appear on people's faces to the head nods that say, "yup, I've been there, too." That's what happens when you live in the borderlands. The tumultuous space in between the worlds in which we reside, the constant conflict we undergo, the feeling of being alone because we're not simply one or the other. We're both.

I now know that I am *also* the English version of my name. The English name has gotten me through my education, it has taught me how to codeswitch, and how to navigate these academic institutions in covert and assimilatory ways. It's allowed me to enter spaces where so many before me were not allowed in.

It's made me "less different" and appeased others' prejudice notions of Brown women. It's helped me survive. And as a result, I have learned how to utilize my access and the privileges afforded by it to benefit those who will come after me, as so many women of color have done for me.

It's brought me to Gloria Anzaldúa and Kimberlé Crenshaw and Tara Yosso. Their work helped me understand that I am not alone in this experience, in this journey, in this life. Their words helped me see that the sacrifices and scars matter. That I don't need to hide or shrink myself to meet someone else's standards. And above all, that I can use what I've learned to help others by sharing my experiences with the intention to make things easier, more accessible, and slightly less violent. I hope that one day my writing will be as healing to someone as theirs have been for me.

And now? Now, I have the power to be my true self. I can accept both versions of me and know that it doesn't make me any less of one or the other. The English doesn't take away from my Mexicanness and the Spanish doesn't make me any less worthy of occupying these spaces. I call upon both when I stand in front of a classroom teaching my sociology classes in predominantly white universities. When I lead workshops and present my research to rooms filled with academics, I am *Marisa*, with the rolled "r" and extended "i." In each of these spaces that were not built for us, I stand as my authentic self, carving out space and making it clear *que aquí estamos y no nos vamos.* I can now correct people when they mispronounce my name and not just let it go. And while I know they won't always get it right, I can expect them to try, to sit in the discomfort at not being able to pronounce something just as so many non-native English speakers experience.

It's a constant struggle, and I know this is not the end of my journey to reclaim my identity. It's a full process of managing my self-doubt, forgiving myself and others, reminding myself that I deserve to live authentically in every space I enter. It's a larger process of showing others that they can demand others to fully recognize them and their cultures, to pronounce their names correctly and not accept "English versions" if they do not want to. The personal is political, it is cultural, and it is valid.

CHAPTER 17

Esta puente/mi espalda

Interseccionalidad entre feminismo y chicanismo

Roxana Fragoso Carrillo

> *Soy una puente columpiada por el viento, un crucero habitado por*
> *torbellinos, Gloria, la facilitadora, Gloria, la mediadora, montada a*
> *horcajadas en el abismo. (...) ¿Qué soy? Una lesbiana feminista ter-*
> *cermundista inclinada al marxismo y al misticismo. Me fragmenta-*
> *rán y a cada pequeño pedazo le pondrán una etiqueta.*
>
> GLORIA ANZALDÚA (1988, p. 165)

∴

Resumen

En los años setenta, a pesar de que el movimiento feminista comenzaba a
posicionarse tanto en la academia como en la sociedad en general, también
fue inicio de una ruptura interna. La teoría feminista, como afirma Barahona
Maldonado (2013), tiene una praxis política que no se puede dejar de lado. Por
esta razón, en la década de los ochenta algunos grupos sociales levantaron su
voz al no sentirse identificados con el feminismo hegemónico que únicamente
problematizaba la condición de la mujer desde una sola categoría. Uno de los
grupos disidentes fue el feminismo chicano, conformado por mujeres hispano-
parlantes residentes en Estados Unidos que eran doblemente excluidas, tanto
por su por su condición de mujer como por su posición racial.

En las siguientes líneas se describirán algunas de las tensiones que han exis-
tido en los últimos años en lo que hoy conocemos como feminismos (agrego el
plural por la diversidad) y su acercamiento con otras disciplinas, en el particular caso, con la literatura. Se estudiarán los trabajos de Linda Nicholson (2011)
y Teresa Maldonado (2013) para imbricar estos apuntes con *Esta puente/mi*
espalda. Voces de mujeres tercemundistas en los Estados Unidos, antología de
cuentos y poemas de escritoras chicanas, afroamericanas y asiáticas residentes
en Estados Unidos, en algunos casos lesbianas en la cual, autoras como Ana

Castillo, Norma Alarcón, Gloria Anzaldúa entre otras, hablan, como ellas mencionan, sobre "nuestro propio racismo".

Más Allá De La Teoría

Como se ha mencionado anteriormente, el feminismo presupone un saber que además de académico tiene sus consecuencias prácticas y políticas, lo que Maldonado (2013) describe como "Teoría y praxis, acción y reflexión son dos polos indisolublemente enlazados" (p. 20), sobre todo si hablamos de un saber que busca derrocar o cambiar el sistema patriarcal. Para conocer el surgimiento del debate entre los distintos feminismos y sus propuestas es necesario hacer primeramente unos pequeños apuntes sobre sus orígenes y desarrollo para analizar cómo han operado en forma de exclusión algunos primeros feminismos.

En las últimas dos décadas del siglo XIX surgió un movimiento anglosajón a favor del voto de las mujeres;[1] sin embargo, el movimiento sufragista "ignoraba la situación de las mujeres blancas de clase obrera, así como la de todas las mujeres negras" (Davis en Maldonado, 2013, p. 29). A este respecto, en *Esta puente*, Cherríe Moraga afirma que "muchas de las sufragistas abandonaron la causa abolicionista cuando se vio estratégicamente claro que debilitaba su oportunidad de obtener el voto para la mujer" (Moraga en *Esta puente*, p. 3). Dentro de las primeras corrientes del feminismo posterior a la segunda guerra mundial se encuentra la obra Betty Friedan en *La mística de la feminidad*, quien cuestiona el rol de la mujer y las características patriarcales que aluden que la mujer pertenece al ámbito privado, es decir, al de la familia y al del hogar. Sin embargo, se le critica que su obra sigue siendo reduccionista y excluyente ya que solo contempla a las mujeres blancas en situaciones privilegiadas.

Tras la publicación del *Segundo sexo* (1949) de Simone de Beauvoir regresa el debate por los derechos de las mujeres y algunas décadas consecuentes, la llamada tercera ola feminista irrumpe en los años sesenta con el debate sobre el concepto de género. Silvia Turbet menciona que la inserción del concepto de género en las teorías feministas "permitió subrayar, por un lado, la ocultación de la diferencia entre los sexos bajo la neutralidad de la lengua y, por otro, poner de manifiesto el carácter de construcción socio-cultural de esa diferencia" (citado en Nicholson, 2011, p. 7). Además de este planteamiento, también se encuentra la postura del feminismo radical que tiene como lema "lo personal también es político" cuestionando la división entre lo público y lo privado en la que se ve inmersa la posición de la mujer. Y es justamente en esta línea que es posible unir el análisis de la antología *Esta puente/mi espalda* reunión de ensayos, poesía y teoría política escrita por mujeres asiáticas, chicanas, indígenas y afroamericanas que debaten alrededor del tema del feminismo las cuestiones raciales, de clase, étnicas así como orientaciones sexuales.

This Bridge Called My Back: Writings by Radical Women of Color título original de *Esta puente/ mi espalda* fue publicado en 1981, editado por Gloria Anzaldúa y Cherrie Morgara y traducido al español en el año de 1988, está compuesto por una serie de ensayos y relatos que denuncian las múltiples exclusiones a las que son expuestas varios grupos raciales y étnicos de mujeres en Estados Unidos, consta de tres secciones una vinculada a la teoría, titulada *Las raíces de nuestro radicalismo*; una segunda parte llamada *Entre líneas* y, por último, se encuentra la sección llamada *Un mundo zurdo*.

Por cuestiones de espacio se retomará únicamente el cuento de *La prieta* de Gloria Anzaldúa, ya que es una de las autoras más representativas de la literatura chicana y permite, además, ver algunas cuestiones de la interseccionalidad en el feminismo. Cabe aclarar que el concepto de la interseccionalidad es retomado de las lecturas de Nattie Golubov (2017) quien la define además de una herramienta epistémica y metodológica como una manera para "detectar las múltiples discriminaciones que se entrecruzan de tal forma que cotidianamente producen la subordinación y la marginación de las mujeres en distintos ámbitos de la vida pública y privada" (pp. 197–198). Es así como en esta antología distintos grupos de mujeres realizan una denuncia a través de la literatura.

En *La prieta* Gloria Anzaldúa, quien, desde su condición como mujer chicana, cuestiona primeramente su ámbito privado para después pasar a problematizar las diferencias ya sean raciales o de género en su contexto social. Gloria E. Anzaldúa es una escritora chicana, nacida en Texas. Fue una de las dos editoras de la primera versión de la antología *This Bridge Called My Back: Writings by Radical Women of Color* publicada justamente en la década de los ochenta en donde varios feminismos convergen en la teoría y comienzan a problematizarse distintas nociones relacionadas a la alteridad.

Específicamente, el texto de *La prieta* es genéricamente un híbrido ya que mezcla prosa que se puede identificar como autobiográfica, con narrativa y poesía. En este relato, Gloria Anzaldúa narra sobre su infancia, cuestiona el papel de su madre durante sus primeros años y también cómo se ha visto desde el seno de su familia como diferente. El rol de la obediencia es una de las constantes de esta obra, además de su posicionamiento como chicana, campesina y lesbiana. "Cuando nací, Mamá grande Locha me inspeccionó las nalgas en busca de la mancha oscura, la señal del indio, o peor, de sangre de mulata" (Anzaldúa, 1988, p. 157), comienza a narrar Gloria Anzaldúa en su relato, dando importancia primero a su propio cuerpo.

En este relato la autora narra la relación que tuvo primero en su familia, lo que podemos entender como el ámbito privado, así como algunas de sus propias tragedias, como el haber sufrido una histerectomía. Esta operación para la autora también está cargada de simbolismos entre el cuerpo y lo que significa ser mujer: "El marzo pasado las fibromas en complot con una infección intestinal se me hicieron como sandías en mi útero. El doctor jugó con su navaja. La Chingada abierta, violada por la vara del hombre blanco" (Anzaldúa, 1988, p. 163). El cuerpo en la teoría feminista se inserta dentro del debate de la dicotomía de los conceptos de sexo/género, mientras que el primero solo es considerado por sus características naturales y biológicas, el segundo se entiende como una construcción social e histórica. Sin embargo, el sexo también está cargado de múltiples simbolismos, parte de la herencia cultural que hemos tenido sobre lo que el cuerpo de una mujer significa. En palabras de Judith Buttler, "la diferencia sexo/género sugiere una discontinuidad radical entre los cuerpos sexuados y los géneros culturalmente construidos" (citado en Nicholson, 2011, p. 8).

La protagonista de *La prieta* se posiciona entre dos culturas, la mexicana y la estadounidense, dice que a pesar de ser descendiente de una familia de mexicanos en Estados Unidos por más de seis generaciones, todavía reside en ellos esa cuestión de verse y saberse inferiores. Gloria Anzaldúa, además, cuestiona cómo los propios grupos étnicos, o minoritarios son quizás los causantes de la reproducción de patrones de racismos, misoginia y otros lastres que venimos cargando con el paso de nuestras generaciones. Algunos autores consideran que este relato se adelantó a su tiempo, ya que apenas se comenzaba a formar en la academia una teoría sobre los multiculturalismos unidos a las perspectivas feministas o de género.

A pesar de que en las primeras líneas el carácter de denuncia sea evidente y también se mantenga un tono pesimista, al finalizar, Anzaldúa propone vencer las barreras de las diferencias a través de la unión, a través de la empatía. La autora deja en claro que el racismo y opresión son una herencia difícil de la cual deshacernos, que es necesario desaprender y cuestionarnos a nosotros mismos como a las instituciones. "Si no creamos estas instituciones, seguramente las perpetuamos con nuestro apoyo inadvertido. ¿Qué lecciones aprendemos del ladrón?" (Anzaldúa, 1988, p. 166) advierte. Este relato, juega entre la autobiografía, que, a modo de confesión abre paso primero, a posicionarse ontológicamente dentro de su familia, para después tomar un lugar en la sociedad.

El relato de *La Prieta* así como toda la obra en conjunto de *Esta puente/mi espalda* tiene como objetivo hacer visible la exclusión de diversos grupos de mujeres, en palabras de Maldonado: "nombrar las cosas es hacer luz sobre ellas. Los conceptos alumbran la realidad en el doble sentido de que la iluminan y le dan ser, la tornan concebible, es decir, pensable" (Maldonado, 2013, p. 21). De esta manera, podemos observar cómo, mediante el ensayo, las intelectuales latinoamericanas y de otros grupos étnicos tuvieron un rol importante en la formación de un feminismo plural que emergía durante la década de los ochenta. A pesar de que han pasado casi poco más de cuarenta años, el debate interno dentro del feminismo aún existe, los movimientos feministas transfóbicos son un ejemplo de ello. Sin embargo, considero que por medio de la academia y el activismo en conjunto se pueden seguir logrando muchos cambios.

El tema de la interseccionalidad dentro de los feminismos aún queda por explorar, pero sin duda, la antología de *Esta puente/Mi espalda* es un buen ejemplo de cómo el esfuerzo colectivo ayuda, como bien se titula este conjunto de obras, a formar un puente entre las diferencias de los distintos movimientos.

Note

1   Un ejemplo es la *Declaración de Séneca Fall*s hecha en el año de 1848.

Bibliografía

Anzaldúa, G. (1988). Esta puente/mi espalda. En C. Moraga & A. Castillo (Eds.), *Voces de mujeres tercemundistas en los Estados Unidos* (pp. 157–168). ISM Press.

de Beauvoir, S. (2015). *The second sex*. Vintage Classics.

Golubov, N. (2017). Interseccionalidad. En H. Moreno & E. Alcántara (Eds.), *Conceptos clave en los estudios de género* (Vol. I, pp. 197–213). Centro de Investigaciones y Estudios de Género de la UNAM.

Maldonado, B. T. (2013). Apuntes para una introducción a la teoría feminista. En C. Díaz Martínez & S. Dema Moreno (Eds.), *Sociología y género* (pp. 19–42). Tecnos.

Moraga, C., & Anzaldúa, G. (Eds.). (1981). *This bridge called my back: Writings by radical women of color*. Persephone Press.

Nicholson, L. (2011.) La interpretación del concepto de género. En S. Tubert (Ed.), *Del sexo al género. Los equívocos de un concepto* (pp. 47–81). Ediciones Cátedra.

CHAPTER 18

Parteaguas

Two Poems & a Story

Juana Moriel-Payne

Expresión

La tarde aferrada a la cocina
afuera amanece
la olla al vapor
cuece sin sal ni romero
sopa de letras caen
del techo cuarteado
con el cierre de la puerta
las vocales
todas abiertas
por miedo
por vergüenza
ahogan una O que quiere ser A
en un abecedario carente de Ň
la palabra claroscuro se revuelve.

Encargos

Las mujeres de mi casa
tejen trenzas largas que enamoran
abren vientres que conciben
cuidan senos que amamantan.

Por encargo del instinto
siembran los ombligos de sus hijos en el patio
—*para que se queden, para que no se vayan*—cantan
mientras riegan los geranios
        lavan el ropaje de las cunas
        bañan las criaturas del mañana.

© JUANA MORIEL-PAYNE, 2022 | DOI:10.1163/9789004521155_019

Del mercado a la estufa se hacen tristes
al alba sirven cafés sabor amaneceres
despiden hombres y mujeres sur al río
y regresan cantando soledades a sus mesas.

Las mujeres de mi casa van muriendo
llaman a los hijos, a las hijas del pasado
—*para despedirnos, para besarlos*—ruegan

Algunos cruzando
regresamos norte al río
escarbamos nuestros patios
para encontrarnos el ombligo
para hallarnos solos, sólo
con las piedras que cargamos.

Anotaciones domésticas

Hilda Ramírez de Gutiérrez llega al puente internacional Santa Fe a las seis y media de la mañana. Se une a la línea de gente que espera, y ni la ambulancia, ni los paramédicos que llegan para aliviar el ataque de asma a su amiga Rosa, la hacen regresar. Tampoco el viento que le golpea la cara con 3 grados centígrados.

Hilda lleva pañuelos en la bolsa. Antes, si le pedían uno, lo daba. Ya no, mucho menos a los hombres ¡Cabrones! Creen que si una mujer, fuerte como ella, les da un pañuelo, quiere cama. Por eso ya no habla con nadie en la línea y cuando llega frente al oficial, sólo responde a lo que le preguntan, "¿qué traes en tu bag?" "Toallas sanitarias"

Hilda camina hasta la camioneta que por dos dólares la lleva a la casa donde le toca hacer la limpieza. De todas prefiere esa, la que tiene un estanque. A la hora del almuerzo se sienta al frente y con el caer del agua y los peces nadando casi se olvida de sus deudas, las que se echó encima cuando pagó el secuestro de su nieto y el funeral de su hermano asesinado en plena avenida Insurgentes.

Hilda lava y plancha ropa ajena como ella, a esa casa de la que no quiere salir. Es tan tibio el ambiente, el sol entra por la ventana de la cocina, mientras lava los platos y toma un té de menta que corta del macetero. Debe terminar a las cuatro de la tarde, pero estira el día. Riega las plantas, lustra el trastero, ordena los libros, acomoda las persianas, busca más quehacer.

Hilda anda por la calle El Paso a las cinco y media de la tarde, con bolsas llenas de encargos: cereal, crayones, golosinas, shampoo y acondicionador y dos galones de jugo de manzana que compró por último en la tienda del dólar, mientras se repite que es fuerte, lo dicen hijas, nietos y el marido, quien la espera del otro lado con cara de hambre. Cuando ella sube al coche, él le asegura que es bien chingona y que tiene antojo de tortillas de harina para la cena.

CHAPTER 19

Beyond Capture

Borderless Embodiments

Kiri Avelar

My creative practice is designed to further provoke thought around the artistic, physical, and cultural borderless experience of Latinx artists in the United States, immersing audiences in unique spaces to explore themes of *ruido*, mestiza consciousness, intersectionality, migration, and *Latinidades* through film, visual art, embodied oral history performances, interactive screendance, and soundscapes.

Figure 19.1, titled *Ruido,* looks at the body as voice and the concept of the body in action as *ruido*. Inspired by the life and work of Boricua Spanish Dance Artist, Sandra Rivera, the castanets represent the connection in diaspora to our colonial heritage, a way of recuperating our inherited cultural practices, crossing the space between our identities in America and the "other side" of the border.

Figures 19.2–19.4 are a series of three images that explore the intersection of the body, food, *cultura*, rhythm, and labor: *Cilantro Taconeo, Manos de Maiz,* and *Texas Masa*. This series considers gestures, symbols, and sounds that speak to the in-between space, and is inspired by the work of Chicana feminist scholar, Gloria Anzaldúa, and Mexican American dance artists Franchesca Marisol Cabrera and Michelle Manzanales.

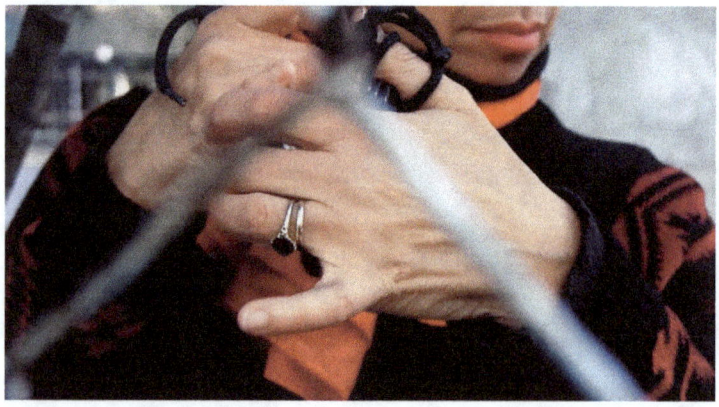

FIGURE 19.1   *Ruido*

FIGURE 19.2   *Texas Masa*

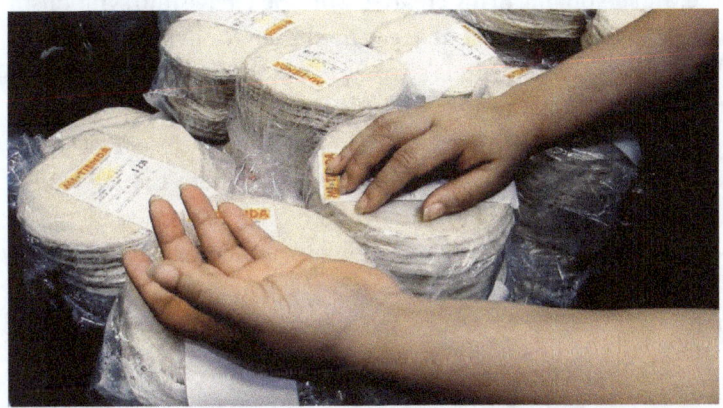

FIGURE 19.3   *Manos de Maíz*

FIGURE 19.4   *Cilantro Taconeo*

CHAPTER 20

Shadow Series

Carol Mariano

Artistic Statement

I have a strong belief that humanity's problem can be resolve through creative dialogue. My approach towards my work deals with contemporary issues of identity and displacement, exploring the idea of the self and its boundaries between the personal and the political. There is a perpetual need to explore the sense of self, place, and belonging in my creative work. So I delve into symbolism by using the shadow as an idea and an image, a metaphor for living in-between cultures. Framing with Gloria Anzaldua's work, the stark reality of "invisibility" examines the angst of crossing over towards being seen—embodying the constant struggle for survival and the ongoing tension about loss and death. It penetrates beyond the physical geographical border where the subjective experience transforms the idea of being in a vulnerable and borderless place. At the same time, the movement between ownership and belongingness seeps through the rough edges. Rewriting the undertow beneath the boundaries of the personal and the political. Always shapeshifting to a different state of being.

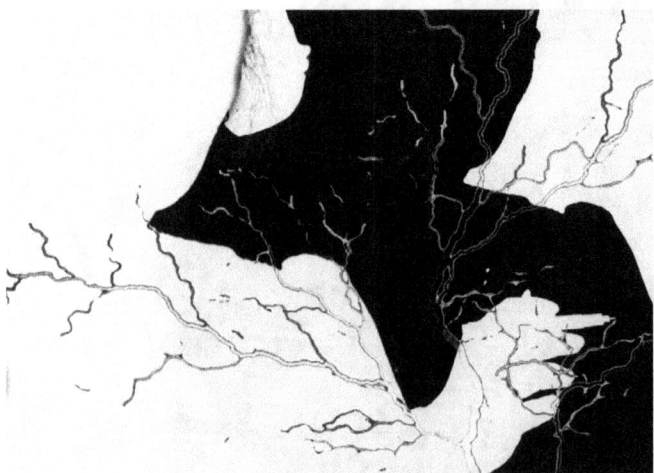

FIGURE 20.1 Shadow 1. This image explores the boundary or intersection between the imaginary self and the real self—an internal and external struggle to rewriting the narrative

FIGURE 20.2 Shadow 2. In this work, the image attempts to depict the uncertainty of its position, perpetually negotiating, challenging, and questioning its boundaries

FIGURE 20.3 Shadow 3. Here, the (imaginary) self-attempts to meander beyond the margin of being "the other," where its meaning is constantly shifting and in motion and where its experience gives birth to multiplicity—the fragmented self—always incomplete

PART 5

Writing as a Sensuous Act

∴

CHAPTER 21

Todo en una maleta

Irving Ayala

No puedo creer que tuve que dejar todo atrás, hasta lo más mínimo que tenía. Cuando tenia 15 años la vida no daba mas vueltas dentro de mi pueblo, era humilde nada particular, un lugar rústico, una montaña en la parte trasera de nuestro pueblo y una particularidad de ese año que no se podría olvidar. Dentro de las actividades diarias era la recolección continua de agua, desde las fuentes de la ciudad; lo recuerdo muy bien. Había un mercado donde mi madre le gustaba comprar nuestros alimentos, siempre muy cerca del anfiteatro. Durante el verano mi madre se condujo hacia mí y mi hermana menor, nos ordenó recolectar nuestros zurrones, añadir un cambio de ropa y buscar por las cosas importantes, tomar una bolsa y guardar unos alimentos, y frutas necesarias para el viaje de unos cuantos días. Teníamos que meter todas nuestras vidas dentro de una mochila. Nunca entendí la razón de nuestro viaje, especialmente las instrucciones creaban más incógnitas que respuestas; aun no entendía lo que significaba un escape. No podía despedirme, no podía interactuar nunca más con nadie con los que crecí. Me negué a acompañar a mi madre y mi hermanita, pero mi madre comenzó a cantar la canción con la que crecí, poco a poco dijo:

> Te voy a proteger,
> cae la noche, se aproxima la oscuridad
> no le voy a conceder,
> el frio no detendrá tu serenidad
> Te entrego mi vida
> a pesar de que nunca te cuestionaré
> aunque este indefinida
> no te fallaré, pero no me detendré
> A pesar del tiempo
> yo te recordaré

En ese momento me di cuenta de la realidad, mi padre nos había dejado ya hace más de seis meses, era el único varón, ellas dos no podrían sobrevivir sin alguna figura masculina, en este mundo las personas piensan que las mujeres no valen nada. Empaqué todo lo que podía necesitar, tuve que dejar cosas que amaba, personas que apreciaba, pero esto era necesario. Aun no conocía la razón de nuestra huida, ni porque teníamos que irnos sin despedirnos; pensé que mi madre había caído en los rumores de que el monte Vesuvius iba a destruirnos a todos, los oráculos solo incitaban miedo.

∴

Dos días dentro del viaje tuve la valentía de preguntarle a mi madre dónde nos encontrábamos y hacia dónde emigrábamos, me respondió que nos dirigíamos a Roma, la capital del mundo, pero en este momento nos encontramos en Nápoles. Nápoles lo conocía, su comida era increíble, pero nos dirigíamos a Roma, en ese momento no lo pude creer, Roma, ese nombre siempre había resonado en mi cabeza desde que era pequeño, era la gran ciudad del emperador. El viaje no fue nada agradable, ya que nos escondíamos de los guardias que no dejaban entrar a nadie a Roma, ya que el emperador Tito había ordenado la entrada y salida de sus ciudadanos romanos completamente prohibida, ya que se encontraba en peligro de guerra y no quería espías, ya que el fuego que el año anterior fue creado, daban índices que las personas fuera de la capital del mundo lo crearon. Mi madre había preguntado a alguien de Nápoles que si nos ayudaba a pasar como esclavos y concubinas para adentrarnos dentro de la ciudad de Roma. Nos encontramos un problema, nuestros disfraces no funcionaron y los guardias y funcionarios públicos de la ciudad nos encerraron en jaulas durante días y nos separaron; la idea de venir a Roma no fue la mejor, odie cada segundo dentro de esa jaula, mi madre ya no se encontraba en el mismo lugar que nosotros, durante ese tiempo creí que la habían comprado para ser una concubina. Éramos solamente mi hermana y yo, ella tenía miedo, yo tenía miedo, pero por eso me encontraba en este lugar para poder darle un poco de consuelo. Comencé a cantar:

> Te voy a proteger,
> cae la noche, se aproxima la oscuridad
> no le voy a conceder,
> el frio no detendrá tu...

∴

Han pasado algunos meses desde que salimos de ese extraño lugar, encontramos a nuestra madre, nos liberamos de la esclavitud, nos dimos cuenta que los oráculos tenían razón, nuestra madre tenía razón. Hacía pocos días que encontrábamos la verdad de nuestra huida, nuestro debilidad, nuestro pecado salvó nuestra vida. La ciudad de Pompeya cayó, el volcán Vesuvius hizo erupción, no era un monte, era un volcán. La destrucción fue tan grande que destruyó todo, la gente no logró escapar, existió mucho caos y mucha muerte, nosotros vivimos ahora para poder contar esta historia. Ahora mi madre, mi hermana, y yo vivimos dentro del estado romano, tenemos una vida que no es la mejor pero no nos podemos quejar. Este cambio no fue lo que esperaba pero he comenzado mi vida en este lugar sin olvidar de dónde yo vengo.

when i say diaspora

José Olivarez

you imagine leaving, you imagine the sound rain makes on aluminum roofs, what producers spend their whole lives trying to recreate on a drum machine, you imagine phone cards, time zone adjustments, translating dollars into pesos, you imagine Western Union yellow as the realest blues there is, i say diaspora & all you see is the trail a plane leaves in the sky, another ellipsis to add to a life full of ellipsis, ribcage ribcage ribcage, you imagine the absence of bird song in the winter, but when i say diaspora i mean roses for every day my mom spent in Mexico and roses for every day since, i mean roses and not the thorns, i mean roses grown in the richest soil, i mean blood is only one way to learn family, i mean my Vietnamese homies and my Filipinx homies and i mean Mississippi diaspora and Louisiana diaspora and yes, i mean mis queridos mejicanos too, i mean anybody who ever knocked my hand away & hugged me instead.

© JOSÉ OLIVAREZ, 2022 | DOI:10.1163/9789004521155_023

CHAPTER 23

La mujer de papa, arroz y yuca

Lina Paredes Espitia

Tal vez en otro tiempo, en esos tiempos donde las doncellas eran vírgenes y los caballeros gallardos, hubiera sido diferente. Tendría hombres a mi derecha e izquierda, propuestas de matrimonio por montones, insinuantes miradas al caminar.

¡Actos de heroísmo se hubieran hecho en mi nombre!

Por mí, se hubieran movido países, mi ser hubiera podido marcar la historia, hubiera podido ser una Cleopatra; sin el suicidio, una María Antonieta; sin ser decapitada o una Marilyn Monroe; sin sobredosis. Tal vez, en otro tiempo, mi ser; hubiera seducido presidentes.

Pero en estos tiempos actuales, mis tiempos, me toca conformarme con un título completamente diferente "una gordita adorable". Y no se confundan, "adorable" no es palabra para describir a ninguna de las mujeres anteriormente nombradas; "adorable" es el término que se usa para cachorros, bebés y abuelos.

Así que ahí me encontraba yo, frente al espejo con un sudadera que luchaba por no romperse y contemplando mi "adorable" ser. En general y para ahorrarme descripciones, sólo digamos que todo lo que tenía enfrente podía resumirse en: redondo y forrado. Suspiré con resignación, otra mañana había pasado y otra vez no había salido al parque "¿Cuál es el punto?" reflexioné acariciando mi estómago. "Lo bien valorado que hubiera sido todo esto en otros tiempos" pensé con la absoluta convicción de que mi sudadera y yo hubiéramos podido conquistar a Kennedy.

Para mejorar la situación estaba, claro, mi ubicación espacial: París. La ciudad del amor y la talla -o. También la ciudad del arte por desgracia. Así que si alguien se preguntaba qué hacía ahí una latina pura sangre, una mujer de arroz, papa y yuca, como yo, en una ciudad donde el prototipo de belleza no le hacía favor alguno, la respuesta es sencilla: aprender a ser una artista y sobrevivir a los tiempos que le tocó vivir.

"Mañana" pensé "Mejor la siguiente semana" reflexioné mejor pensando en dejar el pan y el tinto con azúcar durante ese tiempo. Al final; me alejé del espejo y me alisté para irme. Para cuando llegué a mi clase el hecho de haberme visto reflexionando en lo "adorable" de mi ser, estaba enterrado y con llave en la caja de.

© LINA PAREDES ESPITIA, 2022 | DOI:10.1163/9789004521155_024

"Momentos para no contar a nadie".

Disfruté del olor a pintura al entrar al taller, me acomodé en mi puesto y admiré mi hermoso lienzo en blanco. A él no le importaba la talla de quien lo pintaba, ni sus manos, su cintura o su nacionalidad, sólo le importaba ser pintado ¡Como lo amaba!

—Bonjour Angélica—mi momento con el lienzo fue interrumpido por Sean, sus grandes ojos verdes, y su simétrico rostro me dedicaron una amplia sonrisa, la cual apenas pude devolver. Mis 4 años estudiando francés siendo la mejor de mi clase rápidamente se evaporaron y pude sentir mis mejillas arder.

—Bounjour Sean—le respondió Anastasia, la personificación perfecta de la belleza francesa y la antítesis de todo lo bueno de dicha nacionalidad.

Sean le respondió con la misma sonrisa amplia que me había dado a mí. "Comunista emocional" pensé mientras resignada sacaba mis materiales. Mire una vez más mi lienzo "Tú eres el único que me entiende" le dije con cariño "¿Que dibujaré en ti el día de hoy?" La puerta del estudio se abrió de inmediato, como dándome una respuesta.

Monsieur Jacques entró riendo a carcajadas con dos mujeres en bata, una de ellas, alta, piel marfil y una increíble cabellera crespa, su andar dejaba claro su incomodidad y enojo. La otra, se encontraba riendo incluso con más ahínco, que mi (normalmente) amargo profesor. Ella, tenía la piel morena, cabello largo y ondulado, hermosos y enormes ojos cafés...

—Mon class aujourd'hui, je présents à notre modèles Elena et Katalin

Elena (la rubia, con problemas gestuales) apenas alzó una de sus cejas y nos miró a todos. "Pensar, que por una así se destruyó Troya" pensé al ver la prepotencia con la que nos detalló a cada uno de nosotros con sus increíbles ojos grises. Seguido de esto, tranquilamente se quitó la bata, se dio la vuelta y caminó desnuda hasta una silla, donde se sentó cruzando las piernas. Su cuerpo era lánguido, sus pechos dos firmes gotas con terminación rosa, sus piernas dos columnas interminables, y para mi desilusión, no había ninguna muestra de celulitis, vena varice o en general grasa. "Lo que daría en estos momentos porque a esa silla le faltara una pata" me divertí con el pensamiento por un momento. Luego de haber contemplado aquel pavoneo, no pude evitar sentir preocupación por la otra modelo que permanecía al lado de mi profesor.

Mis ojos se posaron casi con incredulidad en el cuerpo curvo, todavía sin revelar de Katalin. Ella era mucho más bajita que Elena y su bata revelada las grandes curvas de su anatomía, una anatomía que yo conocía muy bien. "Dios mío, no lo hagas" pensé angustiada "Estos no son los tiempos correctos para un cuerpo así" seguía diciéndole a Katalin en mi mente como si la "obesidad telepática" existiera. Katalin había mirado tranquilamente todo el desfile de de Elena, su sonrisa no había disminuido en lo absoluto, sólo cuando ésta terminó en la silla, ella y Monsieur Jacques compartieron una mirada y se rieron.

Luego ella se apartó de él y nos contempló a todos. Sus ojos grandes eran cálidos y afectuosos, su postura era recta y orgullosa "Por favor, huye mientras puedas yo los distraigo" pensé sintiendo un fuerte malestar en todo el cuerpo. Miré a mis compañeros, sus miradas se encontraban atrapadas en los grandes ojos de Katalin, que consciente de que su hechizo había alcanzado a todos los presentes, fue soltando lentamente el listón de la bata. Justo cuando nuestras miradas se encontraron el listón estaba por desaparecer.

Katalin soltó una risa fresca, inclinó su cabeza, me miró tiernamente y empezó a darse vuelta, dejando caer lentamente la bata al piso. Al final se encontraba de espaldas a nosotros, y desnuda. Sus nalgas estaban caídas, con celulitis, pude ver algunas estrías en sus caderas. Volteó su rostro para vernos, su mirada era pícara y su gran sonrisa se mantenía. Luego caminó lentamente hacia donde estaba Elena y se acostó tranquilamente de lado en la base que se encontraba al lado.

Nadie se atrevía a hablar. Su cuerpo estaba lleno de curvas, tenía grandes senos, vientre redondo y prominente, piernas cortas, y brazos robustos; se veía hermosa. Monsieur Jaqueks carraspeó un poco su garganta, provocando así el despertar paulatino de cada persona en aquel salón, que poco a poco, fue tomando su lápiz. Sin embargo yo no sabía muy bien qué hacer.

¿Cómo podía? ¿Cómo lo lograba? ¿Cómo carajos había hecho de esa sala su espacio? Me tomó un tiempo notar a Monsieur Jaqueks a mi lado, apenas nuestras miradas se encontraron, pude notar un fuerte "Qu'est-ce que vous attendez?" cogí por instinto el lápiz, él se dio por bien servido y siguió observando los demás trabajos.

El lienzo que tanto amaba ahora me daba terror ¿Cómo poder pintar lo que estaba observando, si ni siquiera lo entendía? ¿Por qué? ¿No era yo quién decía que era sólo cuestión de tiempo y geografía la belleza? ¿Por qué ahora me costaba tanto retratarla? "Solo muéstrame la verdad" Le dije a mi lienzo y entonces me dejé llevar.

Un rato después, contemplé el boceto una vez más; le había pedido verdad y él me la había dado. Katalin sin pedirle permiso, ni perdón a nadie se denominaba a ella misma y eso cambiaba el como los demás la denominaban. Sin importarle el año en el que había nacido, sin escudarse en lo que los demás calificaban "hermoso", sin desmeritar a la mujer que tenía al lado o a quienes la rodeaban, ella se denominaba hermosa, sensual y una mujer de este tiempo, a juzgar por las miradas que estaba recibiendo, los demás estaban de acuerdo.

Miré mi boceto por un momento. Mi lienzo no había terminado conmigo, algo se sentía familiar en el boceto que había hecho de Katalin sus ojos, habría podido jurar haberlos visto antes, su cabello, sus manos. Cuando por fin lo entendí la verdad me golpeó fuerte en la cara como una cachetada seca pero necesaria. Me levanté de la mi silla y salí caminando rápidamente del salón.

Cuando volví a entrar a la clase, las modelos ya no estaban y la mayoría de gente se había marchado. Me dirigí directo a Monsieur Jaquecks y lo abracé con fuerza, olía a cigarrillo y sarcasmo. El pobre hombre no tenía idea de lo que estaba pasando y para el momento en que mis ojos, todavía rojos por las lágrimas, se encontraron con los suyos, supe que si no lo soltaba, estaría cerca de perder la materia.

Merci—logré decir al final y en su rostro se dibujó una sonrisa casi burlona, casi tierna.

Au revoir, Angélica—me respondió al final.

Sonreí ampliamente, ignoré las miradas escandalosas de los pocos estudiantes que quedaban en el salón y fui a recoger mis cosas. Miré de nuevo el lienzo, esta vez sin ansiedad, me reconocí en él, desnuda, al lado de lo que los demás denominaban "una total belleza". La miré a ella y me miré a mí "Que hermosa estoy" pensé y me reí, esa verdad recién descubierta todavía hacía a mis ojos aguar.

—Au revoir, Angélica—los enormes y un poco confundidos ojos verdes del encantador Sean me sacaron de mis pensamientos.

Agarré tranquila mi mochila, confiada me dirigí a él, le agarré la cara y le di dos besos en cada mejilla, luego todavía con mi mano en su cara le pique el ojo.

—Au revoir Sean

Ante una mirada de fascinación y una sonrisa que jamás le había visto dedicarme, sonreí ampliamente y me dispuse a ir por mi sudadera.

Ya en mi casa, al terminar de cambiarme, me encontré con mi reflejo en el espejo y recordé esta vez sin lágrimas, lo que vi en ese mismo espejo cuando salí del salón por primera vez. Pude ver que mis ojos, eran del mismo color que los de mi madre, mi cabello era del mismo color y forma que el de mi abuela y mis manos eran mías y con ellas podía lograr cualquier cosa. "Tú preciosa, te mereces ser mostrada por todo el parque" me dije; sonreí una vez más, abrí la puerta y pensé "Qué buen día".

CHAPTER 24

Hecho a Mano, "Made by Hand"

Raphaella Prange

There was once a pair of navy-blue boots. Not frilly in any way, more of a boy's than a girl's shoe. These boots tell a story. They have seen many things and felt many years. But amazingly, they look almost new, almost untouched by their history. Even though they were worn by many.

The original owner of these boots *es una niña* who is a second-generation American. The soles of these shoes say "hecho a mano;""made by hand." And this is significant. These shoes were bought in Nicaragua by the immigrant father of the little girl; for his *chica Americana*. And while this little girl did not know it at the time, the shoes and their imprint were to become a symbol of a family of *hermanas*. An encouragement to the little girl to "be made by her own hands."

Esta niña grew up in South Florida as the oldest child of *cinco hermanas*, and she had two artists as parents. They were entrepreneurs and bartered for

FIGURE 24.1

The boots, *Hecho a Mano*

© RAPHAELLA PRANGE, 2022 | DOI:10.1163/9789004521155_025

resources. When one sister needed braces, the father gave one of his prized paintings to the orthodontist. *Esta niña* was an adult from an early age, carting around her *hermanitas* everywhere she went. She was a latch key kid. There was no one to watch her after school. She watched her sisters and they watched her. They either toiled over homework or housework; learning Algebra, reading books, cooking meals, or doing the laundry. But she was always told by her artist father that she could do anything, and she believed him; except to *hable español*. He asked her to hide her heritage, in fear that revealing it would duplicate the hard life he had, a life he fled coming to America. After she grew out of these little boots, her sisters, one-by-one wore them. They were also told that they could do anything, except to *hable español*. And anything and everything they did, except connect to their heritage. It was a chasm that split them down the center as they aged. They seemed to be *hecho por sus propias manos*, but not made by their culture.

The little girl loved school, as it was an escape. Her papa pushed her to do her best and to get out to start her life. She was 16 when she graduated from high school early and went on to college to be a journalist. She never had a *Quinceañera*. She was never to wear the dress or to mingle with her relatives. This sadness laid on her chest, but she wanted to cover people's unique stories—so she went to college far away, in Indiana. She loved stories of people and where they came from. She longed to have her own story. So, in Indiana, on this bright and shiny college campus, she wore blue contacts, and she dyed her hair blond. She never *hablaba español*. She fulfilled her language requirement by taking French. She tried to pass, but it didn't fool people. Her dark roots, her olive skin, and her name revealed her to her Indiana peers. People knew she was different, but she didn't want to be different. She heard her papa say "*ser blanca es tener éxito*". So, she tried to be a white as she could be. She ate cheesy casseroles and pizza—all the things college students ate. But she did secretly miss the mangos, avocados, lechon, and tostones. With each bite of whitewashed food, she gained pounds that seemed to further separate her from her roots.

At the end of her second year of college, her artist parents told her that the money was gone. There was no more bartering to be done. The family home was lost. There was no more money to fund college. None of her friends at college had parents who were claiming bankruptcy, who had to move to the mountains to escape the creditors. She couldn't tell them, in fear that she would out herself even more. Not just that she was Latina, but that she came from poverty as well; that her father didn't speak English well, that she didn't go to high school sleepovers or class trips because she was the family *niñera*. This is why she didn't wear all the new clothes, why she ate so much in the cafeteria, and why she longed to be like everyone else. Not having *deniro* can do that to you—you long to experience what you think others are experiencing. Feeling foreign in your own skin becomes normal, and you believe it is normal.

So, she decided to stay at school and get four jobs. *Ella trabajó y trabajó.* And while she missed her hermanitas so much, she knew she needed to be the example. She became the first person in her family to earn a college degree. She went on to earn a Master's degree. She never moved home. She never spoke Spanish. She only visited. She became an educator instead of a journalist. She was able to tell and appreciate stories in different ways.

Slowly, she began to explore her heritage, albeit privately. Her blond hair became a lighter brown and then highlighted, then darker shades of brown, until it was restored to its natural almost black tone. The blue contacts made their way to the trash, and her brown eyes sparkled naturally. She saw in many of her students similar struggles to harness and love their identities. This became her passion.

Her *hermanitas* followed her path, one-by-one. They made their lives by hand, as well. And the little navy boots went into the attic. The wearers of the boots lived far and wide, and the boots collected dust as they took in the story of the two parents who remained in *la casa en las montañas*. While *las chicas* would come home for holidays and eat rice and beans, plantains, and churrasco—the food would still remain the only cultural connection. The papa never taught or spoke his native tongue. His broken English would become symbolic to the little girl, of all the other things that were broken.

Then a call came one day. *La madre* had cancer, and, less than 6 months later, she passed away. All the little girls, now grown, continued to make their lives by hand. No *hubo* funeral. There was too much grief. The little navy boots were joined in the attic by the mother's high heels. And while the father beamed with joy with each hand made step *sus hijas* made, there was still much grief there. The original little girl began to wonder about *Dias de los Muertos,* and her relatives in Central and South America. She mustered up the courage to speak broken Spanglish on trips to Florida and at the local Mexican mercado. The little girl, now a woman, began to feel connection. She began to understand that her success came from her roots, not in spite of it.

The father began selling shoes. Was this coincidence? Every time the little girl went home, she was surrounded by shoes and was reminded of her father's hand-made life and, the mother, whose name labeled the store. She began to encourage the four other little girls to connect to their past and present. Some were ready, some were not. Still, today, she is the only one who tries to *hable español.*

Ahora las padres se han ido. The father was taken by his own hand, as his little girls were making their lives by their own hands. The little girls converged on the shoe store to clean things out, a lifetime of handmade items and legacy. They opened the attic. The original owner of the shoes took them to her own home, for her own daughter—*una hija que lleva el nombre de la madre.* But the boots were *demasiado pequeña.* Maybe this demonstrates that this new little girl cannot be bound by *estos zapatos solos,* that her culture is bigger than what can fit in these little soles. But these boots continue to be a reminder of how far the little girls have gone and the care that has been taken to preserve the legacy of many years. Perhaps they will fit a great granddaughter someday, and the story can be passed on to her. She can continue the legacy of making her life by her own hand, but supported by her rich heritage *en español.*

My reader, I leave you with this parting thought: *Los recuerdos son la arquitectura de nuestra identidad.* Let the memories in your soul and pass them on so others can understand the importance of our history and culture. *Sanamos compartiendo.*

CHAPTER 25

La Chip Truck

Felipe Quetzalcoatl Quintanilla

Es que tu padre siempre ha tenido brillantes ideas. Siempre se ha quedado con las ganas de abrir un negocio, por ejemplo, pero el problema, *dice mi madre*, es que no tiene la disciplina. Acuérdate nada más lo que pasó con la chip truck.

¿No te acuerdas cómo estuvo eso? Todo comenzó cuando el Pastor Guido nos contaba maravillas sobre la ciudad, o más bien pueblo, de su esposa. Una zona rural famosa, nos contaba, por importar miles, y estamos hablando de generaciones, de mexicanos para trabajar cada verano en los invernaderos de tomates y flores. Una zona tan llena de mexicanos que el gobierno de México tuvo que abrir ahí un consulado porque los de Toronto nomás no se daban abasto. Tantos mexicanos que cuando Los Tigres del Norte vinieron a tocar a Canadá, no llegaron a Toronto ni a Montreal, date cuenta, no, no, vinieron a Leamington, Ontario Canadá.

Y nos quedaba a una hora y media de Sarnia. Entonces fuimos a darnos una vuelta, y sí, antes de entrar al pueblito se veían ya esos invernaderos gigantes, los paisanos prietitos por el sol pedaleando sus bicicletas por la autopista rural. Ya llegando al mero Leamington, veíamos a los compas caminando por el parque central, uno que otro con su esposa canadiense e hijos mexicano-canadienses disfrutando de una caminata dominical.

El Pastor Guido, te acordarás, nos llevó a conocer a la familia de su señora. El suegro era un mexicano de esos que había venido cada verano a Leamington desde los finales de los años 60s, de esos que le había trabajado tan bien a su patrón, que éste no tuvo otra que sponsorear para traerlo a vivir *full-time* con todo y familia. Bueno, el señor, un patriarca a estas alturas, había jalado ya a una cantidad de muchachos de su pueblo natal de Hidalgo, a seguir sus pasos.

La hija leamingtoñena, a saber dónde o cómo fue que conoció al Pastor Guido, pero pues por esas cosas del destino ahí estamos nosotros, caminando por un auténtico pueblito mexicano canadiense, aunque les pese los Canadienses que no se hayan acostumbrado a los morenitos a tal punto. Bueno, fuimos a ver qué comíamos por el pueblo. En esos tiempos, notamos que solamente había un solo establecimiento, un bar, que servía comida mexicana y que manejaba una familia italiana. Los muchachos iban cada fin de semana a echarse sus tacos, pero más que todo a escuchar música y ahogar sus nostalgias en pitchers de cerveza. A desahogarse con sus compañeros, o comprar el cariño de una mujer, y terminar la noche montándose en sus bicis tambaleantes, arriesgando la vida en autopista, para llegar a dormir algunas horas antes de levantarse a trabajar.

Bueno, fue ahí que le vino la idea a tu padre de abrir un restaurante auténticamente mexicano en el mero Leamington, Ontario, Canadá. Obvio, no teníamos el dinero para iniciar semejante empresa, pero ese era el sueño y tu padre, entonces, tuvo otra idea, *¿y qué tal si comenzamos con una chip truck?*

Y bueno, ahí me tienes, porque siempre soy yo la que ejecuta las ideas de tu padre, ahí me tienes buscando pa' arriba y pa' abajo, los chip trucks en venta por todo el sur oeste de Ontario. Finalmente, encontramos un anuncio de una chip truck que vendía un canadiense de Sarnia por $8 000 dólares, lo cual sonaba como bastante buen *deal*, ¿no? Fuimos a ver la santa *chip truck* y sí, en efecto, ahí estaba, medio maltratada, necesitaba algo de trabajo, cambio de carburador, batería o algo así, la cocina asquerosa, pero la parrilla y el sistema de ventilación se veían nuevitos. El dueño la tenía en los afueras de Sarnia, aparcada con un rótulo de *For Sale*, al frente de un junke. El hombre era un de esos típicos canadienses que nunca se cambian para salir de casa, pelo largo pero ya calveando, y la barba sucia. Pero bueno, el canadiense decía que ya tenía una nueva chip truck y que por tanto quería deshacerse de esta, que era por otro lado, una súper oferta si la queríamos y la aceptábamos *as is*, lo cual es canadiense, para "así como la ves y a mí ya no me metan después".

Tu padre se emocionó, y bueno, yo también cuando consultando con una casa de préstamo, veía que quizás sí lo podríamos lograr. Nos prestaban $6 000, eso sí, con un interés gigantesco, pero como te dije, para entonces tu padre y yo ya estábamos bien emocionados y en verdad pensamos que iríamos a Leamington a recoger dólares como si fueran las hojas de los árboles en otoño. Pues ahí vamos a aceptar el préstamo a lo bruto y todavía ni alcanzábamos a reunir los $8 000, pero tu padre tuvo la idea de decirle, bueno, que yo le dijera, al canadiense que le podíamos dar $5 000 ahora y 6 pagos de $500 de aquí a tres meses, ¿ves?

Bueno, al canadiense se le iluminaron los ojos. Que sí aceptaba, dijo, pero, eso sí, que se quedaría con el *ownership* de la *chip truck* hasta que le diéramos el último pago. Qué solamente nos daría una fotocopia, si la queríamos y nos servía. Y ahí sí a tu padre se le activaron las antenitas y me dijo que no, que mejor buscaba otro chip truck por otro lado. "Este cabrón nos quiere ver la cara de pendejos, Dolores. Nos va a salir con una mala jugada," decía.

Pero yo por acelerarme, y porque en esos tiempos todavía estaba como en una luna de miel con los canadienses, pensando que todos eran personas honestas y buena gente, me acuerdo que le rogué y le dije que "no, Mario, no te preocupes. Los canadienses no son así. Él no nos va a salir con ninguna babosada. Ten fe en las personas". Y bueno, el chiste es que sí le dimos los $5 000 dólares y él nos dio las llaves de la chip truck y fotocopia del ownership que no nos servía, en realidad, para nada.

Bueno, pues el problema inicial con no tener el ownership es que no se podían procesar las placas para circular y entonces a donde quiera que quisiéramos llevar la bendita *chip truck* nos tocaba pagar grúa. Bueno, pues ahí vamos con grúa al taller de Rigo. Y sí, efecto, Rigo, ya sabes, siempre nos ha tratado bien y le hizo las reparaciones requeridas por $200 o algo así. Y de ahí hasta Leamington, OTRA vez en grúa.

Habíamos encontrado, según nosotros, el mejor lugar para poner la *chip truck*. Según nuestras investigaciones de campo, los trabajadores iban a hacer sus compras al *No Frills*. Llegaban en bicicleta o en vans que sus patrones les proporcionaban para que fueran y vinieran todos juntos los fines de semana. La idea era que los trabajadores verían que alguien finalmente les estaba preparando tacos auténticos con aguas naturales de horchata, fresa y tamarindo. Tu padre, tú sabes, tiene un buenísimo sazón y la idea era prepararles tacos exquisitos y baratos. Hablamos con el manager del *No Frills*, y este sí se portó bien, la verdad. Nos dejó parquear la *chip truck* afuera de su establecimiento y hasta nos dio acceso a la electricidad y el agua, todo gratis. En fin, llevamos la *chip truck* para allá. Y bueno, ustedes se acordarán de esto, íbamos a las tortillerías de Detroit y a comprar nopales, queso Oaxaca en mayoreo en el mercado de La Colmena en *Little Mexico*. Ya en el *No Frills*, y para consumirle al manager, comprábamos la carne y cilantro, cebolla, todo lo demás. Tu padre se ocupaba de la carne. Preparaba tacos de lengua, de carnitas, suadero, al pastor. Y yo de lo demás. Y cuando ustedes iban, te acuerdas, tu papá te ponía a cortar el cilantro y la cebolla y tus hermanos a algunas otras cosas por aquí y por allá, como las aguas o cuidar las tortillas... y yo las relaciones públicas. O sea que cobraba, servía y daba las probaditas.

Bueno, para nuestra sorpresa, los mexicanos simplemente no nos hacían caso. Llegaban más que nada los poquitos canadienses que se atrevían a probar los *true tacos mexicahnoos*, y otros cuantos que se desilusionaban al darse cuenta que en efecto no vendíamos ni papas fritas ni poutine ni hot dogs ni nada que usualmente se espera uno encontrar en una chip truck.

Ahí fue que tu padre tuvo entonces otra idea. Preparaba mini tacos, bocadillos y probaditas de las aguas, para darles a los que venían saliendo de la tienda. Y ahí íbamos tú y yo y tus hermanitos, cuando iban, detrás de ellos. ¿Te acuerdas? Y sí, los muchachos probaban y agradecían y sonreían y preguntaban de dónde éramos. Pero pues nada más no nos compraban.

Entonces tu padre tuvo OTRA idea: que teníamos que ir a las granjas mismas para hablar con los muchachos y convencerlos.

Y hasta eso, fíjate que los granjeros sí nos dejaron hablar con los muchachos. Entrábamos a esas casas portátiles, te acuerdas, donde vivían entre 10 a 20 muchachos, por la noche ya cuando se ponían a escuchar música, ver televisión, y tomarse sus dos tres cervezas antes de dormir. Y nos sentábamos a platicar con ellos. Nos contaban de qué parte de México venían, cuánto tiempo hacía que venían, sobre sus hijos y esposas allá. Nos ofrecían parte de su cosecha, ¿te acuerdas? que salíamos cargados de tomates y otras cosas.

Y bueno, pues tu padre ya con unas cervecitas les hacía el *hardsell*, ¿verdad? Y que "miren, muchachos, nosotros les preparamos buenos tacos y a buen precio. Además si nos compran, les damos un *ride* de vuelta cuando terminen de hacer sus compras". Y bueno, los muchachos sonreían y se sonrojaban un poquito, daban las gracias y decían que sí, que así lo harían.

Pero al final no dio muy buen efecto la estrategia. Sí nos llegaron a comprar algunos de ellos y les llegamos a dar sus *rides* de vuelta a sus granjas. Pero fueron muy pocos los que se atrevieron. Y al final, lo que nos sorprendió fue otra cosa, y es que poco a poco vimos que se sí estaba levantando el negocio, pero que era, más bien, con los menonitas de la zona. Es decir, con los descendientes de los menonitas que habían partido de Canadá para Durango, Zacatecas, San Luis Potosí, en los años 20, porque aquí el gobierno les había negado la posibilidad de hacer su propio *homeschooling*, y de pronto se habían topado con la estricta obligación de enviar a sus hijos a la escuela pública... situación que iba completamente en contra de su cultura. Bueno, pues los descendientes de esos migrantes que estaban ahora regresando a Canadá por eso de la violencia, pues, eran ahora completamente bilingües, y tenían experiencia en el campo, y por tanto se conseguían trabajos de supervisores en las granjas. Bueno, todo esto para decirte que estos menonitas sí que comenzaron a comprarnos más que los otros compatriotas. Y era chistoso, porque llegaban las parejitas con sus tres o cuatro hijitos, todos güeritos, ojos azules, vestidos tradicionalmente, en sus camionetas negras con tremendas calcomanías de águilas devorando serpientes sobre un nopal, y su música norteña, a todo volumen, y te llegaban a pedir sus tacos de lengua en perfecto norteño mexicano... y pues parecía que finalmente se estaba levantando todo, más o menos.

Al principio íbamos de jueves a sábado. Bueno íbamos y regresábamos. Tú ya sabes, hora y media de camino. Yo le decía a tu papá que lo que teníamos que hacer es quedarnos a dormir en Leamington y estar, de hecho, toda la semana. Pero tu padre, que ya estaba un poco desilusionado, nunca quiso quedarse allá y dormir en la *chip truck*. Prefería su cama. Pero el problema con eso es que me tardaba yo mucho en levantarlo y convencerlo que saliéramos y casi siempre llegábamos pasando la hora de lunch y bueno era un relajo.

Lo que más desanimaba a tu padre es que los compas no nos compraban y pues esa había sido la intención... Pero bueno, me acuerdo que una noche fuimos con algunos de ellos que ya eran conocidos, al famoso bar del italiano. Los muchachos ya estaban en plan de relajarse y llenaban el establecimiento pidiendo las Coronas por cubeta. El propietario les ponía la música de su tierra por satélite y algunos, ya con algunas copitas, se ponían a bailar. Nosotros nos sentamos con un señor, de esos mayores que tienen años yendo y viniendo, respetado por todos sus muchachos. Platicábamos de la vida en Canadá, y después de un rato nos contó cómo estaba la cosa para ellos. Cómo, reciente- mente, acababan de atropellar a uno de sus compañeros cuando iba en rumbo a casa en bicicleta y cómo el conductor simplemente se esfumó. Que estaban precisamente reuniendo dinero entre los compas para enviarlo de vuelta a México. Que sí, por ejemplo, ofrecían clases gratuitas de inglés para ellos en el centro comunitario pero que después de 12 horas de trabajo quién iba a tener ganas de aprender inglés. Qué lo más difícil era estar lejos de las esposas y los hijos y no verlos crecer. O lo opuesto, contaba, que también había aquellos que se habían encontrado a alguien acá y se habían olvidado de sus mujeres e hijos allá. Y eso sin hablar de cómo se los bailaban acá las canadienses del bar.

"Mire a esa gordita canadiense que está bailando con esa compa." Nos decía. "Ya varios la conocen. No habla español, solo sabe decir 'guapo,' 'papa- cito,' 'garra qui, garra lla'. Y los muchachos que bailan con ella, pues luego no encuentran la cartera, ¿ve? Y ella, 'no, pues yo no fui, yo no sé'. ¿Y pues uno qué le va a decir a un policía con su mal inglés? ... Nada, verdad."

Pero, bueno, no todo era así de triste, nos contaba. Muchos de ellos tenían ya sus terrenitos allá, con sus casitas y tiendidas que cuidaban las esposas. Muchos de ellos tenían hijos que iban o habían ido a la universidad, licenciados, profe- sionistas en México...

Bueno, pues estábamos ya entrados en la conversación cuando tu padre tocó el tema de la *chip truck*, y el señor sí se sinceró con nosotros. "Mire, Don Mario," nos decía, "yo le agradezco mucho lo que nos ofrece usted y su señora, y que piense en nuestros muchachos. Pero, pues para serle honesto... la verdad no creo que le vayan a consumir. Todo el dinero que ganan o lo envían para México o lo gastan en cerveza o aquí con mujeres. Nosotros mismos compramos torti- llas y latas de frijoles y otras cosas y ya con eso hacemos nuestras comidas para el lonche y la cena. Tenemos un comalito en casa y ya con eso la llevamos..."

Fue como un balde de agua fría que nos había echado ese señor. Pero curio- samente él mismo fue quien nos dio el aliento, y la siguiente gran idea: porque otra opción que quizás sí podría funcionar era cuando los muchachos salían del bar, "ahí sí salen siempre con un montón de hambre, y yo a esa hora" nos decía, "ya no les tengo nada en casa para prepararles".

Bueno, pues ahí vamos, tu padre y yo, emocionadísimos, a hablar con el italiano. Y sí parecía que todo fluía. El tipo no tenía ningún problema con que pusiéramos la *chip truck* afuera por la noche. El plan que se iba vislumbrando, entonces, era lo siguiente: vender entre semana afuera del *No Frills* a los menonitas y canadienses y por la noche a los mexicanos, al frente del italiano, los fines de semana. El único problema con esto, y era uno grueso, es que aún no teníamos las placas ni el desgraciado *ownership*, y pues no podíamos andar pagando grúa cada vez que nos tocara movernos, ¿verdad?

Fue entonces que tu padre me mandó a hablar con el dueño de la *chip truck*, y tú fuiste conmigo, ¿te acuerdas? El *driveway* lleno de carros viejos y la entrada de su casa repleta de envases de cerveza vacíos y basura. Le tocamos la puerta un rato y salió el canadiense sentándose a fumar ahí en las escaleras al frente de su casa. Tenía los shorts de mezclilla, sucios, todos rotos y se le salían los testículos. Qué asco y qué vergüenza me dio... contigo sobre todo. Bueno, pues le empiezo a decir lo que habíamos practicado con tu padre. Que teníamos ahora el lugar perfecto para vender tacos a los mexicanos que salían borrachitos y con hambre de un bar. Que claro que le pagaríamos todo lo que faltaba pero que para poder hacerlo teníamos que tener el *ownership* para sacar las placas y entonces poder mover la *chip truck* entre los dos lugares que teníamos. Que le firmaría todo lo que quisiera ante un notario o abogado pero que por favor nos ayudara para poder pagarle. Pues seguro que te acuerdas que este idiota nos respondió todo agresivo y con su sonrisita, que "no, no te lo voy a dar. De ninguna manera haría tal cosa," y que solamente nos entregaría el ownership, hasta que le termináramos de pagar hasta el último centavo. Pues ese fue un poco el final de esa fabulosa idea. Simplemente, no íbamos a poder movernos al frente del bar hasta que pudiéramos pagarle todo todo al canadiense. Y, pues, no nos tocaba de otra que seguir al frente del *No Frills*, y ver si solamente con los menonitas y canadienses funcionaba la cosa.

Llevábamos dos meses en ese trance, con tu padre ya tan desanimado, que no se quería parar de la cama, ni manejar hora y media para llegar a darles de comer a los uno que otro canadiense y menonitas, ni darles probaditas a los mexicanos.

Pues precisamente uno de esos días que llegamos más o menos tarde al lugar nos encontramos con que, ¡Zás!, la chip truck ya no estaba ahí. El manager del *No Frills* nos explicó que había llegado un hombre que tenía los papeles del camión y las llaves y que como dueño que era, le había informado, se llevaba su vehículo de vuelta. Pues, ya conoces a tu papá, ahí mismo se enojó muchísimo y que "¡viste Dolores! Te lo dije que este cabrón nos iba a jugar chueco" y etc.

Nada y que vamos a la estación de policías donde al parecer ya nos estaban esperando. Ay hijo, cómo nos trataron... como ladrones, que porque nosotros éramos los que nos habíamos robado la chip truck, para empezar, y que podían ahí mismo meternos presos por eso. Fueron tan déspotas y groseros que no tuvimos de otra que salir de ahí todos descorazonados y de vuelta para Sarnia.

No... no, no terminó ahí el asunto. Don Toño, el mariachi salvadoreño, nos recomendó que habláramos con su cuñado que era abogado en un bufete de abogados en Toronto para ver si podía él hacer algo por nosotros. Y sí, este señor fue a corte por nosotros, y el proceso se tardó como dos meses más, y gracias a él, obligaron al canadiense a devolvernos la *chip truck* de vuelta, y nosotros ya no teníamos ni que pagarle lo que faltaba. Pero igual teníamos que pagar la deuda con la casa de préstamo, más lo de su servicio del abogado. Y nos tardamos muchísimos años en pagar todo eso...

No, ya nunca regresamos a Leamington con la *chip truck*. Para entonces tu padre y yo ya nos quedamos con un mal gusto en la boca. No.. la pusimos en venta, y se quedó todavía como 6 meses ahí sobre la *London Line*, hasta que alguien nos ofreció $3 000 por ella, y tu papá dijo que sí, que ya la diera en eso.

CHAPTER 26

West Coast Paisa

Julio Enríquez-Ornelas

solo jeans

they were the coolest pair of jeans in 6th grade. we sat around, near the basketball court, talking about the colors we would get them in and where we could find them. we talked about who had them or how we'd wear them. i said to them, i'd get them in navy blue and i'd wear them with a white hanes t-shirt, a black belt with my initials in the buckles, and some black on white nike cortez. we dreamed of wearing the gear the tough guys wore in our neighborhood. some of us even talked about our uncles, cousins or brothers, and the respect they got dressed with their crisp, clean, and creased jeans.

on weekends, 'ama would take me to the mall or to the indoor swapmeet on alisal street in salinas, california. once, at the swapmeet, i remembered one of my friends said his brother told him they sold solo jeans for $19.99 there. that day with 'ama i searched and searched for my navy blue solo jeans. when i found them, and asked 'amá if she'd buy them. she refused to buy them. she was against them. she ignored me and said, no. i could not understand. they were a good price. she'd bought me pants at this price before. it didn't make sense. so, i went up to her and asked her, "why not? why aren't you going to buy me those pants?" she just said look at those levis or wranglers and told me to pick a pair from that stack. so, i did.

weeks later, at the mall, i found a pair of loose baggy pants, that looked like solo jeans, so i stole them just like 'ama had taught me for our survival a few years back, and i proudly wore them around the house. as soon as 'ama saw me, she was upset. she said you better wear those pants with a belt all the way up to your waist. i ignored her. she didn't understand. some of my friends were allowed to wear solo jeans and dress with hanes t-shirts and nike cortez; it was not fair, i thought. they get to dress how they wanted. their mothers weren't telling them what they can and can't wear. i thought to myself, my uncle *brownie* always gets to wear what he wants.

as i got older and went from middle school to high school, i began to understand why. it all made sense. i walked to school with my click of non-solo wearing homies, carrying our binders stuffed with our pencil pouch, white paper, and divider tabs. we never took the shortcut to school; through the backfield

© JULIO ENRÍQUEZ-ORNELAS, 2022 | DOI:10.1163/9789004521155_027

and then the little sidewalk behind the new houses, because there was a small alley where some of the solo-wearing guys would kick it and every time we walked through there shit could go down. instead, we always took the long route, all around the new houses *por la banqueta*. we'd tell each other we preferred that route "'cause through the field you get mud, grass, and water on our pants and shoes."

one morning, as we walked to school, we saw what happened to *grumpie*. we' d known each other since back when we lived in los padres apartments. he was just a few years older. by now everyone knew him as *grumpie*. he used to be so funny and easy going; he was always drawing stuff. his mom, at times, would invite us home to share a meal, but when we all moved to the apartments on paseo grande, the new and nice low-income housing, he stopped hanging out and changed.

now on the corner of paseo grande and towt street, we walked by him; he was wearing a pair of navy blue solo jeans, a white hanes t-shirt, a black belt with his initials in the buckles, and some black on white nike cortez. two other guys who were roughly wearing the same thing cornered him at around 7:30 am on the driveway of one of those new houses. we saw it all. *grumpie* swung first, and the bigger guy went at him. *grumpie* didn't back down. *grumpie* got him in the face and soon after kicked him, but the bigger guy's homie saw he needed help. so he came up behind *grumpie* and knocked him down, and once on the floor they both kicked *grumpie* over and over, again and again, and *grumpie* just tried to cover-up his face, while he laid on the ground in a fetal position. then the skinny guy pulled out a lanyard full of keys from his big solo jean pocket and started to hit him in the face.

as this played out, we continued our path to school, trying to watch, but keeping our distance; we whispered amongst ourselves should we back him up? should we help him? and one of the santo brothers said "'na fool, it's not worth it, they'll come after you later, and you'll get caught up in it." so we kept on walking to school, and we did not say a word. by then, we were about 14 years old or so. we were all worried and afraid for what we had seen. i remember just wanting to get behind the school fence and out of the street, even though the street was quiet, nice, and well maintained.

once we arrived we went to the cafeteria for breakfast and we still didn't say a word; a few minutes later raúl walked in. he'd normally walk to school with us, but on this morning he woke up late. so out of breath, red and a bit perplexed, he said to us "fools did you see *grumpie?* two *norteños* kicked his ass, he was bleeding all kinds, all over his face, man fool did you guys backed him up? he's one of the homies." we listened, and no one answered. A few minutes later, one of the santo brothers asked raúl where *grumpie* was at, and he responded, "i think he went home 'cause he was walking back to the apartments."

a few months later we heard, he was a big tagger for a *sureño* gang and someone from the rival gang had it after him. they eventually shot *grumpie* and left
him in a coma, and soon after he got better, his parents moved out of town
without telling anybody, something about a witness protection program. we
heard they all moved to one of those far away states where solo wearing dudes
go to when they're tired of wearing solo jeans.

Over sopes and burritos

Back in the early 2000s, my options after high school were Hartnell Community College in Salinas, California or California State University, Monterey Bay,
which meant paying $5,000 in cash each semester. Then, Nubia Martinez told
me as I sat in her guidance counselor office,
   —"you should apply to private colleges"
   —to which I asked "why Mrs. Martinez?"
   —"Because they have private funding, so they can provide aid to undocumented students like you unlike public schools...you don't qualify for state or
federal aid, so it would be too expensive for you." So, I did. I applied to liberal
art colleges all over the United States ranging from Indiana, Oregon, Missouri,
Nevada, California, Hawaii, Colorado to Illinois. My top choice was Santa Clara
University in California. The only public school I applied to was University of
California, Santa Barbara. From both, I received a small envelope with a single
sheet of paper, stating an "unfortunately" of some sort. Yes, it was hard. Yes, I
was disappointed. Yes, I was nervous about applying to college, sin papeles.
   But then, little by little, acceptance letters rolled in from those out of state
liberal art colleges. I was surprised 'cause truth be told I was never a straight A
student. None of the acceptances came with a full ride or at least an affordable
price tag, and I imagined it was 'cause of my average grades. And I knew then my
job as a busboy at Sly McFly's in Monterey Bay was not enough to cover costs.
   But then it all changed one day, after school, while at swimming practice at
Alisal High, my name was called over the school intercom. I had to report to
the main office, and my immediate reaction was...
   —"y ahora qué pasó en la casa." So, worried, and expecting the worst, I hur-
ried, soaked in my swim trunks and flip flops, I walked into Mrs. Martinez's
office and she said with a paper in her hand, "look what just came in the fax." It
had been months since I had applied to this small school in Indiana, back then
it was 1 of 3 all male schools where one could earn a B.A in the United States.
But, I didn't know that back then.
   —So I thought, "Finally, I heard back from this one small private school in
Indiana named Wabash College."

—She said, "it's an acceptance letter with a semi-full ride, expect something in the mail from them, soon."

—I replied, "Wait, are you sure? Do they know I'm undocumented? Do they que no tengo papers? Do they know I'm not sure when my case will be resolved? Do they know I don't qualify for loans? How am I going to get there? Can I fly with my Mexican ID?..." From there I forget the rest. I remember she said this is good news, perhaps she said it due to my inability to discern good from bad news. I remember smiling for the first time in a long time, I remember going back to practice feeling as if I had just won a race at a swim meet.

Later, when the decision had to be made. When the deadline for the deposit to attend was coming up, I remember being all stressed 'cause I had no idea where I was going to get $100 for the deposit. I knew mom couldn't do it. I knew she didn't have the money for that. So, I remember we were at grandma's house in Salinas with a bunch of tía's visiting her, and mom told them how worried I was about the money and explained to them que por eso I was "bien triste."

—So, my tía Silvia said, "yo te prestó 'mijo no te preocupes ya luego me lo pagan." So that day my tía saved the day. Months or weeks later after earning my first round of tips as a busboy, my tía Silvia came over to visit grandma, by then I was already living with grandma, and she asked about the $100.

—I asked abuelita, "should I pay her or wait for mom to do so?"

—grandma said, "como veas 'mijo pero tú mamá siempre anda bien gastada."

—Y respondí, "pues le voy a pagar entonces abuelita, ella me prestó el dinero que ganó limpiando hoteles, no es justo no devolverle su dinero."

Not going to lie, part of me wanted to keep the $100 that I had just earned to buy the important things to an 18 year old. The other part of me was also thankful for her gesture of support. Hasta la fecha, I don't know how I was able to go from the West to the Midwest. It's what I need to do.

Years later in Decatur, Illinois, I share this story with Santiago Vásquez-Vaquera over sopes and burritos before his talk to my Latinx students at Millikin University, and he tells me,

—"You were a pre-dreamer...."

—and I said, "i guess, i could be?"

My first language is Spanglish

If you ask me to not speak Spanglish, or point out how my use of language is deficient. I hear don't use your voice. Silence, I utter for many years because of it.

I'd turn my Spanglish into an only English or only Spanish sign within me. Never both, my academic success early on in school came from learning to build a border within them. It was unexpected when one appeared out of place.

Working to adjust and make a triangle fit into the space of an oval, or a square is exhausting and frustrating. But I tried.

My English and Spanish are borrowed. I had no ownership of either. I already had my language. It was just not allowed. Like when Spanish wasn't allowed in Texas in the 50s like that one Chicana told me one morning as I sold her a burrito in Spanish at the Sunday morning farmers market in Salinas, California.

• •

What should have been a brief dialogue became more than that. She tells me as I intentionally over-stuff and wrap her breakfast burrito, "Spanish wasn't allowed once", to me her statement seemed outrageously unimaginable, especially in Salinas. But nonetheless I throw in extra salsa in her bag. Perhaps to say with my action, "it doesn't matter I still see you", perhaps to say, "I'm sorry that wasn't my experience." Perhaps to say, "I'll overcompensate with salsa on behalf of institutionalized racism everywhere."

She tells me with joy, "I'm glad you speak Spanish, when I was younger they'd hit you with a ruler over your hand for saying your name in Spanish or speaking Spanish in school." She tells me all this in shattered Spanish, proudly. I wanted to say to the Chicana, "my teachers used Spanish. I was in bilingual education up until third grade. In high school, I took Spanish because mom said it was important to always speak Spanish. And I listened. In high school most of my teachers spoke Spanish, many of them came from the community, and they made a point to share their struggle, all while pushing their radicalized Chicano mindset onto us, making the CSU and UC system proud."

• •

When they tell me of how Spanish was banned, I'd often say to myself, "but that's not my experience because you're here, you came back to teach us." So, I thank them in my mind every time. But then when Trump won, speaking Spanish in public became risky.

• •

For years, I'd use my Spanish or English as my own.
For years, I'd claim Spanish as my first language.

For a while, when people ask what I spoke first,
I'd say "I don't know but I imagine Spanish."

Truthfully, in my memory there isn't a time where one didn't exist without the other.
    My English could not be, without its Spanish. They feed off each other. They always lurk and follow each other around. One might interject in the middle of a thought because there was no other way to say it.

It's like both grew intertwined
like the roots of the trees in Lago de Camécuaro en Michoacán.

For years I'd learn to stop one language from interjecting the other when it was speaking. They all had their time to be, this always depended on the receptor of language.
    From the beginning I've known my first language, I was just not allowed to use it because it was misunderstood and scared others. Now, I realize that's not my problem, if they can't communicate with me in my first language, it's their loss, not mine.
    In the meantime, I'll keep saying, my first language is Spanglish.

    dolar

Disolvamos, fronteras, gritaron
los restos en el desierto.
            es que para mi entre el amor y la violencia siempre hubo un muro.
                         Una línea
                       Bien marcada
                          cuerpos
                            caen
                         en la cima
                       Del cielo,
                       Del rio,
                       La tierra,
                       El humo
                        El aire,
                       En polvo,
                       la nada.

Y así como si nada hubiera pasado
ni nadie hubiera visto
seguimos
marchamos
rumbo a
la línea

What if we dissolve borders? Not remove or bridge or break down, but dissolve. Let›s dissolve the border. Disolver. To solve. To breakdown (mentally?). Like grains of sugar consumed in warm water, se disuelven. Until it›s presence is only known by taste, and no longer sight. Escapar de lo visual, sugar. Bebamos pues como si fuera limonada en el verano en algún estado húmedo en las Américas del Norte. Así como Beyoncé.

Disolvamos, fronteras,
gritemos
en el desierto

> At the border
> I scream
> Both sides are my land.
> Both sides are home.
> I carry both, always.
> I am both.
> This highly politicized and contested plot of land is home.

And as I come to pay respects to all of those who have crossed it, I can't help but be overwhelmed in thought with emotion.

> Like visiting sacred lands.
> Like visiting ruins or temples.
> As I walk around this land on All Saints' Day;
> one day after Halloween;
> one day before Day of the Dead,
> I think of all the souls who have died trying to cross it.
> And I ask myself, is this where love ends
> or is it where it begins for thy neighbors?
> Where one country ends or the other begins?

I finally made the pilgrimage, yet,
I'm not allowed to step foot on the sand.
This is our sacred land.
This is our mecca.
This is our promised land.

Disolvamos, fronteras, gritaron
los restos en el desierto.
los restos en el desierto.
los restos en el desierto.
los restos en el desierto.
los restos en el desierto.
los restos en el desierto.

Y así de un país a otro nomádicamente
we carry on entre la violencia y el amor
en la línea.

Coloniality Incarnate

Conversational Assemblage with Liliana Conlisk Gallegos,
Jorge Omar Ramírez Pimienta & Julio Enríquez-Ornelas

Carmella J. Braniger

> As a socially produced and contested space, the U-S/Mexico border
> is coloniality incarnate.
>
> HERNÁNDEZ (2020, p. 5)

∴

C: I'm going to just say a tiny little bit about myself, so you can kind of get a sense of who I am and why I'm doing this project. And then I'd like to just back off and listen to the conversation.

C: I grew up in Trumpland USA and I [quickly] grew tired early on of the rhetoric and the culture. I've always been renegotiating my relationship with my upbringing, I guess. I've spent the last 25 years of my life leaving that place in a way.

> Only something which continues to hurt stays in the memory. (Nietzsche, 2006, GM II 3)

C: I want to recognize that I am an outsider in many ways and I feel like my role and the contribution I want to make to this anthology is one that would show that I want to listen, that this is not about me. This is about you.

L: Can I say, Carmella, you're talking about how you're an outsider. I guess, tambien, me too, even in the border in Tijuana, even then I felt as an outsider and especially particularly in the literary and artistic circles they don't know me but it's not like I'm not part of the show you know, so I can relate in that sense right?

L: We're intersectional beings, right? So we do have our forms of privilege as well, even if we come from the poorest country or the most horrible experiences in life, we still have certain privileges that we don't necessarily wear on our face.

> Intersectionality is concerned with the relationship between power and knowledge production.

J: Building on the work of Gloria Anzaldúa, I definitely want to rethink what borderlands mean in a global context and I think one of the things that's really exciting about this project. We had such a large number of submissions from all over the world. In so many ways, what I expected was chicanos and chicanas talking about the border and we have that, that's the heart of the book.

J: But we had this global phenomenon in response to the call ... now we have a series of different writers, different voices, many of them women who are thinking through Anzaldúa in a global way. So it's almost like how Anzaldúa or even how the spectacle of the border is seen outside of a North American context.

J: The way this project came to be is I posted – I do a lot of sort of passionate-slash-angry posts on Facebook – and I did one that was sort of a poem, called "America, Are You Great Again?" It was right when they were going to do one of those raids for dreamers, and I wrote this poem or what read like a poem, and I think it really spoke to Carmella and that's sort of how the focus of this book came to be, from a writer's post and an interested reader.

L: Thank you both for sharing space here.

O: You know, maybe a couple of weeks ago, I was doing this interview with these poets, and one of the things that I pointed out is that at the border there's this eternal sense we are foreigners, like we are, everyone, even the people that are Kumeyaay, right, have been constantly perceived as the other, as being a foreigner even in their own land . .every border artist is a foreigner because they explore both logics of the border.

O: And in the end, they don't function well within any of the national logics and they end up being the border creator-poet-writer-artist-photographer-academic.

C: Art draws the outsiders into these two logics or even more than two logics. Art makes you able to operate amongst various paradigms, which takes some creativity.

O: Yeah. I mean, just think of yourself as being punk by nature, just by geography. So, I mean, there's a uniqueness that we should pretty much acknowledge, right? I mean, functioning out of these colonial traditions and nationalists approaches. But again, it's really hard to function in larger logics, like academia ... Soon enough, those logics are not going to be as effective.

L: Things are changing.

J: It's all connected to access, knowing opportunity. Cause if you don't know how to function in those circles, you are excluded. Or if you're not sure how to function within that logic, like perform an expected role.

C: But the way in is to learn the paradigm or the logic of the other ...

L: ... and then use that

C: to resist.

L: The thing is, people have historically had to adapt the methods or the formats, not so much the content, but the formats have continued to live on. Right? That's what you see in my painting you are publishing. You see a format, but that's the format of resistance ... we're discovering, we're rediscovering what happened in the past as we move toward the future .... Our past is more like the future because of that.

O: [at the border] these two logics are there. Yes. We can learn them, but it is a lot of work and there it is, it is a system that is, it's a machine that lasts way longer than any given life ... many of the border artists and scholars and writers have to get really creative .... they build their own systems and find their own ways to show and find their own ways to publish and find their own publications to do their scholarly work in. And, and I find that good, but it doesn't mean that I don't have an issue with all these nationalists' two-sided or even multiple-study mechanisms.

L: ... the 500 years plus that we've been living under these systems that are defined by both gender and race .... Like the way that we define beauty, what we think is beautiful, what we think is holy, what we think is worthy of being quoted, right? Those things come from that establishment yet, what Omar said is true. For example, when you read my chapter, I talk about crossing the border every day and not just crossing the border everyday, but crossing the border as a woman that is read as not white. Right? But I'm like, they don't know who I am. They don't know that I come from the water. They don't know the bullshit I went through every day. That training that I have, what I've seen, this is nothing ... it's like I've been trained to kill.

J: I'll bring the gas ...

L: ... turn up the match, man. And burn it all down.

> You must be ready to burn yourself in your own flame. How could you rise anew if you have not first become ashes? (Nietzsche, 2006)

C: I felt that spirit of yours in the piece that you submitted. And I have to say that like, I mean, I'm not trying to just make you feel really good or anything, but when I read your piece, I had the same kind of feeling about the work that I did when I was reading Gloria Anzaldúa for the first time.

J: Where do you think that courage comes from? From your community, from your family, from a writer?

L: It comes from my family history. My great grandpa was in the Mexican Revolution when he was nine years old. He was one of the children of the revolution ... I have a great grandfather-uncle, who just passed away this year. He knows some Kumeyaay, he remembers the language from his grandmother singing to him. And he's around the age of my grandma. So like that's how we know a lot of the little hidden parts of our history.

But in terms of my great great grandpa, he was one of the defenders of Baja, California. So I heard the other side of the story, the "gringos" were killing us, destroying everything, trying to take our houses, trying to get property. People today claim that the defenders got in the way of a true anarchist revolution but that is BS! I'm sure if that happened Baja would belong to the US by now. And then my great grandma, Aurora López Pantoja, was a woman that was very feared. They would call her "La China". And that's what they call people who had Afro curly hair. Right? So she was Black, Indigenous, and possibly European as well and she suffered the stigma of being called a witch.

She was mixed, but she, well she lived in a ranch with all her kids, and her husband would leave them by themselves because he had to go to work. She carried a shotgun, ran a bar, and she grew up and later brought her children up in that circumstance where she had to be a badass. So she fought and was never afraid and she was even blamed for killing a man once. He had a heart attack because the man was so humiliated and angry that a woman would talk back to him. He killed himself! That's where I get my lengua de machete from.

So I think it's the stories that I've heard from my grandparents, parents, and the family. I know that we never gave up. We would be like, okay, but our time will come. Like that idea of resistance, this is the story of resistance. I believe that it's in the genes. I think that my courage is inherited ... And also that I'm just like, I don't wanna say I'm not afraid, but I don't care if people get mad or triggered. I'm not staying quiet. I'll fix it later. Like that. That's how I think.

O: But you say something really interesting and it's the, like this filter, right? People, I mean, your case, my case, I have, I know other people that are incredible border artists, scholars, and writers. But they're the few. The big minority fall through the cracks. It's super difficult. I mean, if you don't have that support. I mean, you're eight years old. Get up at four, trying to get to school at six, seven. You're falling asleep in your classes, I mean, you know you don't belong, and are there only because you have put down an aunt's address or someone else's address. And you're like, I'm committing a crime here, sitting down and trying to learn. Many of us end up just believing that we're criminals. So someone can understand the two broken logics, but might not have the resources, the support ...

L: or clarity, or the mental context ... someone has to open a door for you. Someone has to support you. Someone has to help you ....

O: yeah. There's so many elements. And having that capacity to navigate two logics . . being someone that can look at the two broken logics, you would think, right? ... You would have, I mean, being bilingual, right? You would think you would have more resources.

But you don't.

O: Yeah, and I mean, you're a writer, so there's also this constant search for the correct word. And then if not, I mean, metaphors, and then you bring out some other literary tools to get out of it.

L: Just like that, the script

O: 10,000 pages to one short story,

L: It could have been a sentence.

> In sum, coloniality is the epistemological and material scaffolding for
> the social construction and reproduction of the nation-state boundaries
> and identities and of national, racial, and sexual borders. Such an under-
> standing, in turn, sheds a distinct light on the U-S/Mexico border, as it
> foregrounds the racialized/sexualized nature of violence on the border as
> being grounded in a colonial enterprise and epistem that manifests itself
> in local struggles. (Hernández, 2020, p. 11)

C: I just keep coming back to the two logics we started with. And I think that
what I hear you saying is that there's a certain amount of shifting between
those logics that being a border crosser requires, like there's this extra layer of
being, even; it's not just this extra layer of work, but the shifting, the shifting of
the being under duress. I don't know if burden's the right word ...

O: Yeah. I mean, I'm now examining nomadism as a part of my own language
for explaining my work, because this perpetual not being part of something
has a term, right. And it's a term that has historically been perceived as dangerous and that falls outside of the logics of state, right.

> ... in a state of perpetual transition, the mestiza faces the dilemma ...
> which collectivity does the daughter of a dark-skinned mother listen to?
> (Anzaldúa, 2007, p. 100)
>
> I don't know what to do / two states of mind in me. (Sappho, translated
> by Anne Carson)
>
> This is her home
>   this thing edge of
>   barbwire. (Anzaldúa, 2007, p. 35)

L: So one of the pillars of Coloniality, which is the perpetual revamp of colo-
nialism, right, is binary thinking? Binary thinking is one of the pillars, like over-
simplification is another one. Decontextualization is another one. Hierarchical

organization is another. So there's several pillars of Coloniality. Like Omar said, we're thinking under the premise of nations, but at the same time there's an interdimensionality beyond the nations, and then there's the experience of the self in that space that has been divided as nation and that experience is maybe something you'd rarely or never hear about.

> This land was Mexican once
> was Indian always
> and is.
>   And will be again. (Anzaldúa, 2007, p. 113)

L: My last life is ending right now. Right now. I'm dying from the violent experience of coming to live in the Inland Empire six years ago, starting as a Woman of Color professor here and getting tenure and entering my sabbatical.

L: I have another publication that's going to come out. About how we lose our children. We lose our children to the seas, to the desert, to war, to lack of healthcare, and due to this lack some cannot be born and also mothers die with them in childbirth. We lose our women and children, from the children that are forced to cross the border to the mothers that we're bringing in. And then they are separating them, and all of us the children, from Mother Earth and life. Mother Earth is losing children to these borders.

J: Earlier when we were having the conversation ... of the duality or belonging to two spaces and, and being a nomad, I was thinking about my own experience and my own family. And I've always said that I'm an academic nomad. I just go where opportunity takes me. But interestingly enough, now that I got tenure, for the past six years I was surviving and I knew the limits of what I was expected to do and not do. And I stayed, was stuck, within those boundaries, but that's exhausting.

L: Even if we have some privileges, that doesn't mean we've been having the spotlight or even a space.

J: Right, and the way white power preserves itself is by reminding us that we don't belong and encouraging us not to submit ourselves to the community. I want to make my presence known, and I want la Casa Rosa to become a celebration for me being homesick.

J: the U S Mexico border ... it exists in global cultural memory.

References

Anzaldúa, G. (2007). *Borderlands: The new Mestiza.* Aunt Lute Books.

Carson, A. (2002). *If not, winter: Fragments of Sappho.* Vintage Books.

Hernández, R. (2020). *Coloniality of the U-S/Mexico border: Power, violence, and the decolonial imperative.* The University of Arizona Press.

Nietzsche, F. (2006). *The Nietzsche reader.* Wiley-Blackwell.

www.ingramcontent.com/pod-product-compliance
Lightning Source LLC
Chambersburg PA
CBHW071517100726
47908CB00004B/1191